P9-DBI-197

RACQUETBALL

Steps to Success

Stan Kittleson, PhD
Augustana College
Rock Island, Illinois

Leisure Press
Champaign, Illinois

796.343
KIT

Library of Congress Cataloging-in-Publication Data

Kittleson, Stan, 1934-
    Racquetball : steps to success / Stan Kittleson.
      p. cm. -- (Steps to success activity series)
    Includes bibliographical references (p.).
    ISBN: 0-88011-440-1
    1. Racquetball. I. Title. II. Series.
  GV1003.34.K55 1992
  796.34'3--dc20
                                 91-11908
                                   CIP

ISBN: 0-88011-440-1

Copyright © 1992 by Leisure Press

All rights reserved. Except for use in a review, the reproduction or utilization of this work in any form or by any electronic, mechanical, or other means, now known or hereafter invented, including xerography, photocopying, and recording, and in any information storage and retrieval system, is forbidden without the written permission of the publisher.

Acquisitions Editor: Brian Holding; **Developmental Editor:** Judy Patterson Wright, PhD; **Assistant Editors:** Julia Anderson, Dawn Levy, and Kari Nelson; **Copyeditor:** Wendy Nelson; **Proofreader:** Karin Leszczynski; **Production Director:** Ernie Noa; **Typesetters:** Kathy Boudreau-Fuoss and Marcia Witbeck-Wildhagen; **Text Design:** Keith Blomberg; **Text Layout:** Tara Welsch; **Cover Design:** Jack Davis; **Cover Photo:** Will Zehr; **Line Drawings:** Tim Offenstein; **Court Diagrams:** Gretchen Walters; **Printer:** United Graphics

Instructional Designer for the Steps to Success Activity Series: Joan N. Vickers, EdD, University of Calgary, Calgary, Alberta, Canada

Leisure Press books are available at special discounts for bulk purchase for sales promotions, premiums, fund-raising, or educational use. Special editions or book excerpts can also be created to specification. For details, contact the Special Sales Manager at Leisure Press.

Printed in the United States of America   10 9 8 7 6 5 4

Leisure Press
A Division of Human Kinetics
P.O. Box 5076, Champaign, IL 61825-5076
1-800-747-4457

Canada: Human Kinetics, Box 24040, Windsor, ON N8Y 4Y9
1-800-465-7301 (in Canada only)

Europe: Human Kinetics, P.O. Box IW14, Leeds LS16 6TR, England
(44) 532 781708

Australia: Human Kinetics, 2 Ingrid Street, Clapham 5062, South Australia
(08) 371 3755

New Zealand: Human Kinetics, P.O. Box 105-231, Auckland 1
(09) 309 2259

Contents

The Steps to Success Activity Series is a breakthrough in skill instruction through the development of complete learning progressions—the *steps to success*. These *steps* help students quickly perform basic skills successfully and prepare them to acquire advanced skills readily. At each step, students are encouraged to learn at their own pace and to integrate their new skills into the total action of the activity, which motivates them to achieve.

The unique features of the Steps to Success Activity Series are the result of comprehensive development—through analyzing existing activity books, incorporating the latest research from the sport sciences and consulting with students, instructors, teacher educators, and administrators. This groundwork pointed up the need for three different types of books—for participants, instructors, and teacher educators—which we have created and together comprise the Steps to Success Activity Series.

The *participant book* for each activity is a self-paced, step-by-step guide; learners can use it as a primary resource for a beginning activity class or as a self-instructional guide. The unique features of each *step* in the participant book include

- sequential illustrations that clearly show proper technique for all basic skills,
- helpful suggestions for detecting and correcting errors,
- excellent drill progressions with accompanying *Success Goals* for measuring performance, and
- a complete checklist for each basic skill for a trained observer to rate the learner's technique.

A comprehensive *instructor guide* accompanies the participant's book for each activity, emphasizing how to individualize instruction. Each *step* of the instructor's guide promotes successful teaching and learning with

- teaching cues (*Keys to Success*) that emphasize fluidity, rhythm, and wholeness,

- criterion-referenced rating charts for evaluating a participant's initial skill level,
- suggestions for observing and correcting typical errors,
- tips for group management and safety,
- ideas for adapting every drill to increase or decrease the difficulty level,
- quantitative evaluations for all drills (*Success Goals*), and
- a complete test bank of written questions.

The series textbook, *Instructional Design for Teaching Physical Activities*, explains the *steps to success* model, which is the basis for the Steps to Success Activity Series. Teacher educators can use this text in their professional preparation classes to help future teachers and coaches learn how to design effective physical activity programs in school, recreation, or community teaching and coaching settings.

After identifying the need for participant, instructor, and teacher educator texts, we refined the *steps to success* instructional design model and developed prototypes for the participant and the instructor books. Once these prototypes were fine-tuned, we carefully selected authors for the activities who were not only thoroughly familiar with their sports but also had years of experience in teaching them. Each author had to be known as a gifted instructor who understands the teaching of sport so thoroughly that he or she could readily apply the *steps to success* model.

Next, all of the participant and instructor manuscripts were carefully developed to meet the guidelines of the *steps to success* model. Then our production team, along with outstanding artists, created a highly visual, user-friendly series of books.

The result: The Steps to Success Activity Series is the premier sports instructional series available today. The participant books are the best available for helping you to become a master player, the instructor guides will help you to become a master teacher, and the teacher educator's text prepares you to design your own programs.

This series would not have been possible without the contributions of the following:

- Dr. Joan Vickers, instructional design expert,
- Dr. Rainer Martens, Publisher,
- the staff of Human Kinetics Publishers, and

- the *many* students, teachers, coaches, consultants, teacher educators, specialists, and administrators who shared their ideas—and dreams.

Judy Patterson Wright
Series Editor

Preface

This book is based on my experience and experiments with finding the ways people best learn. The methods and drills have been developed through many years of teaching and feedback from students. I believe you learn faster by doing. All the steps and drills are designed to get you into games and game-like situations as soon as possible. Learning a new game shoud be fun and exciting. It can be more fun if you have success. Every step and drill is designed to help you experience that success. Perhaps the most unique aspect of this book is the attempt to build basic strategy into the learning process at the outset. The six basic rules of strategy will serve you well all your days of playing racquetball.

This book may surprise you if you have used other books to learn other sports. Most start with complete explanations of the history of the sport. Many have lengthy sections on equipment and clothing and explain fundamental movements in great detail.

I have included some of this basic information, but I assume that you have already decided to try the sport—otherwise why would you be reading this book? Another of my assumptions is that you are in a class led by a teacher or have decided to try racquetball at the insistence of a friend, and that therefore you might not own the equipment you are using. If you like racquetball and decide to purchase equipment, a sporting goods store can provide you with detailed information about equipment. When you've become a fanatic racquetball player, you can find books on the history and other aspects of racquetball at your library. A short list of racquetball books is provided at the end of this book to get you started.

This book is designed for players at the beginning level. Every fundamental and shot is developed from the basics. Some advanced shots are not covered. Doubles play is not discussed except as it applies to a game for three players. In spite of this, the book can take a singles player to a very high level of play, so even if you have played some racquetball, the drills and strategies may help you analyze your game and raise it to a new level.

This book's focus is on learning the basic skills and shots of racquetball in the most natural and logical progression. You can use this book in any setting, private or public, and learn the game the way most people learn— by participation and immediate feedback from results or a friendly observer.

Because racquetball is a relatively new sport, there has been a lot of growth in the way the game is played and learned. Many players have learned the game without the benefit of formal classes or teachers. *Racquetball: Steps to Success* can be used as a manual for teaching yourself the game. All you need is a court and a partner. As you gain experience and skill, you can further improve by observing others, asking questions, and perhaps even taking a lesson.

As one who has been teaching racquetball from the time it started becoming popular, I have had the pleasant experience of refining and recording my teaching style. I hope that others will learn and come to love this game that is so much fun and such great exercise. The instructor's manual (*Teaching Racquetball: Steps to Success*) that I wrote to accompany this book presents the same drills and methods of teaching as you'll find here, so if you are in a class, you can expect your teacher to use this book's drills and evaluations in a way that will be very beneficial to you.

There are a great many people to thank for their assistance and support. I am grateful to Human Kinetics Publishers and their staff for the opportunity to share my love of racquetball with others. I want to thank the students of Augustana College for all the feedback and knowledge I have gained, and the research I have had to do, in teaching them. A special thanks to my racquetball partner, Ben Newcomb, for all the lessons I have learned from him. Thanks to Laurel Taylor, Greg Stolze, and Cheryl True for computer assistance, proofreading, and general suggestions. Finally, thanks to my wife, Judi, for her support during the entire process of teaching and writing.

Stan Kittleson

The Steps to Success Staircase

Get ready to climb a staircase—one that will lead you to become a skilled racquetball player. You cannot leap to the top; you get there by climbing one step at a time.

Each of the 18 steps you will take is an easy transition from the one before. The first few steps of the staircase provide a solid foundation—you will practice the techniques of basic, single skills. As you progress further, you will combine the single skills together in ways they are typically used in game situations. As you refine your physical skills, you will also learn game-play concepts as you apply the skills and combinations in modified games.

As you near the top of the staircase, the climb will become easier, and you'll find that you have developed a sense of confidence about your racquetball abilities that makes further progress possible and playing the game a real joy.

To prepare to become a good climber, familiarize yourself with this section as well as ''The Game of Racquetball'' and ''Preparing Your Body for Success'' sections for an orientation and in order to understand how to set up your practice sessions around the steps.

Follow the same sequence each step of the way:

1. Read the explanation of what is covered in the step, why the step is important, and how to execute or perform the step's focus, which may be a basic skill, concept, tactic, or a combination of the three.
2. Follow the numbered illustrations in the Keys to Success that show exactly how to position your body to execute each basic skill successfully. There are general parts to each skill: preparation (getting into a starting position), execution (performing the skill), and follow-through (finishing the action). The numbered items listed are the major points you should focus on for each part.
3. Look over the common errors that may occur and the recommendations for correcting them.
4. Read the directions and the Success Goal for each drill. Practice accordingly and record your score. Compare your score with the Success Goal for the drill. All Success Goals assume that you use the correct form as described in the Keys to Success. Because the drills are arranged in an easy-to-difficult progression, you need to meet the Success Goal of each drill before moving on to practice the next one. This easy-to-difficult sequence is designed specifically to help you achieve continual success. The drills are set up to provide you with purposeful practice and enough repetition to help you improve your skills.
5. As soon as you can reach all the Success Goals for one step, you are ready for a qualified observer—such as your teacher, coach, or trained partner—to evaluate your basic skill technique against the Keys to Success Checklist. This is a subjective evaluation of the quality of your basic technique or form, and it is important because using correct form can enhance your performance. Your evaluator can tailor specific goals for you, if they are needed, by using the Individual Program form (see the Appendix).
6. Repeat these procedures for each of the Steps to Success. Then rate yourself according to the directions for ''Rating Your Total Progress.''

Good luck on your step-by-step journey to developing your racquetball skills, building confidence, experiencing success, and having fun!

Key

S = server
R = receiver
RHR = right-handed receiver
LHR = left-handed receiver
P = player
O = opponent
⊙ = target for ball to hit
⟶ = path of player
--→ = path of ball

The Game of Racquetball

Racquetball is relatively new on the sport scene. In spite of this, it has become one of the most popular recreational sports played today. In the last 20 years, racquet clubs have popped up everywhere, and facilities are available in most moderate-size communities. Colleges and YMCAs have also contributed to the expansion of facilities, so that almost anyone can find a place to play.

Racquetball originated in several evolutionary steps rather than a single event. It might descend from such ancient games as jai alai, handball, and tennis. The most recent history traces its evolution from paddleball at the University of Michigan. Earl Riskey is credited with developing paddleball in the 1920s and 1930s. He reportedly got the idea while watching tennis players practicing in the handball courts in the wintertime. Joe Sobeck is credited with creating the final stage when, in 1950, he added a stringed racquet to increase velocity and control. Whatever the case, we thank these early thinkers for giving us a game that is easy to learn and lots of fun. The purpose of this book is to teach you the game of racquetball. You can consult some of the suggested readings at the end of this book for further details about the history of the game.

ABOUT THE GAME

Racquetball can be played by two, three, or four players. In *singles*, two players oppose each other. In *cutthroat*, two players play as a team against the server; players rotate upon loss of serve so that all have a turn of service, and each keeps her or his own score. *Doubles* competition involves a team of two players against another team of two.

Racquetball can be played on a one-, three-, or four-wall court. Most of the information in this book will be directed toward play in a four-wall court, but many of the principles, drills, and shots can also be used in a one- or three-wall court.

BASIC RULES

You should learn the game of singles first. It starts with the server bouncing the ball on the floor while standing in the service zone (see Figure 1). The serve must strike the front wall first and rebound to the floor behind the short line before touching the back wall. The rebound may hit one side wall after hitting the front wall, as long as it lands in the backcourt before touching any other surface (ceiling, other side wall, back wall). If the ball should strike two side walls, the ceiling, or the back wall or land on the short line, it is called a *fault* and the ball is not in play. The server then receives a second service attempt. Two consecutive service faults result in a *side-out* (often called an *out*) and the server becomes the receiver. Service faults do not accumulate. Once the ball is put in play, the fault no longer exists. The server continues to serve as long as he or she scores points. A service attempt that strikes a surface other than the front wall first is not a fault but an out. No second service

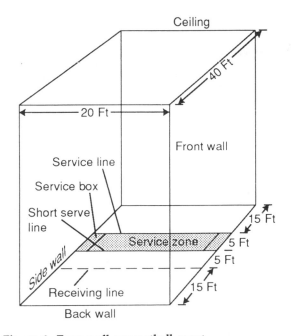

Figure 1 Four-wall racquetball court.

attempt is allowed, and server and receiver exchange places immediately.

The receiver should be stationed in the middle of the backcourt. The receiver may not strike the ball until after it has passed the short serve line, and may not move in front of the receiving line until the ball has crossed the short serve line. The receiving line is marked by a broken line 5 feet behind the short line, but it may not be present on all courts. The rules require that a 6-inch line be marked on the side wall where the imaginary receiving line would end. The receiver may hit the ball in the air (*volley*) or after it bounces once. If the serve touches the floor twice before the receiver can return it, it becomes a dead ball, and the server wins a point (*ace*). The receiver returns the ball to the front wall, but unlike in the serve, the ball may strike any other wall (but not the floor) before striking the front wall. Play continues (*rally*) until one of the players fails to return the ball to the front wall before the second bounce. A point is scored if the receiver fails to return the ball. An exchange between server and receiver occurs if the server fails to return the ball. Cutthroat rules will be covered in Step 14. The scoring system is the same as for singles.

SCORING

Only the server can score points, and the server continues serving as long as she or he scores. It is possible for the server to score 15 consecutive points without the receiver ever scoring. An official racquetball game ends when one player or team scores 15 points. There are no ties or requirements to win by two points. In tournament play, a match consists of the best two of three games, with the third game (if necessary) played to 11 points. You may encounter modifications of these scoring systems. Some people play the best three out of five games to 11 points. Some play games to 21 points.

PLAYING RULES

Following are the most important rules, for your reference. Only the most important rules

that pertain to learning the game are listed. For a complete copy of the rules, write to the American Amateur Racquetball Association (AARA), whose address is given at the end of this section.

Points and Outs

Points are scored only by servers when they serve an ace or win a rally. The server loses the serve (*out*) when he or she loses the rally or makes two successive faults.

Serving

The serve shall not be made until the receiver is ready and the server or referee (if present) has called the score.

Fault Serves

There are five common types of fault serves. Any two in succession result in an out.

1. **Foot fault**. If the server does not begin the serving motion with both feet within the service zone, or steps over either line before the served ball passes the short line, it is a foot fault. The server's feet may touch but not extend over either line.
2. **Short serve**. This is any served ball that first hits the front wall and on the rebound hits the floor on or in front of the short line (with or without touching a side wall).
3. **Three-wall serve**. This is any served ball that first hits the front wall and on the rebound hits both side walls on the fly (before bouncing on the floor).
4. **Ceiling serve**. This is a serve that first strikes the front wall and then touches the ceiling (with or without touching a side wall).
5. **Long serve**. This is a serve that first hits the front wall and then strikes the back wall before touching the floor (with or without touching a side wall).

Out Serves

There are six common types of out serves. Remember that an out serve means that the server is out immediately, even if no prior fault exists.

1. **Missed ball**. Any attempt to strike the ball that results in a total miss or in the ball touching any part of the server's body.
2. **Non–front wall serve**. Any served ball that does not strike the front wall first.
3. **Touched serve**. Any served ball that touches the server or her or his racquet on the rebound from the front wall.
4. **Crotch serve**. Any served ball that hits the crotch of the front wall and floor, front wall and side wall, or front wall and ceiling is an out serve. A serve rebounding to the crotch of the back wall and floor is good and in play. A served ball rebounding to the crotch of the side wall and floor beyond the short serve line is also good and in play.
5. **Illegal hit**. Contacting the ball twice or hitting the ball with the handle of the racquet or any part of the body or uniform is an illegal hit and thus an out serve.
6. **Fake or balk serve**. This is defined as any noncontinuous movement of the racquet toward the ball as the server drops the ball for the purpose of serving. Any feint or false attempt to deceive the receiver results in an out serve.

Dead Ball Serves

A dead ball serve is neither a fault nor an out. There is no penalty, but it does not cancel a prior fault. There are three common types of dead ball serves.

1. **Screen ball**. When the serve passes so close to the server that the receiver's view of the ball is obstructed, it is a screen serve. The call is made by the receiver if no referee is present.
2. **Court hinder**. If the serve hits any part of the court that under local rules is designated as a court hindrance, it is a dead ball serve.
3. **Broken ball**. If the ball is determined to have broken on the serve, it is a dead ball serve.

Rallies

Each legal return after the serve is called a *rally*. Here are the most important rules that apply to rallies.

Legal Hit

Only the head of the racquet may be used to return the ball. The racquet can be held in one or both hands. Switching hands to hit a ball, touching the ball with any part of the body or uniform, or removing the wrist thong are illegal and result in loss of the rally.

One Touch

On a return, the ball may be struck only once. The ball may not be "carried." (A carried ball is one that rests on the racquet momentarily so that the effect is more of slinging or throwing the ball.) This violation loses the rally. However, if you swing and miss the ball, you may continue to attempt to return the ball until it touches the floor for a second time.

Failure to Return

It is considered a failure to make a legal return if the ball bounces on the floor more than once before you hit it, or if the ball does not reach the front wall on the fly after you return it. If your return strikes your opponent and obviously did not have the force or direction to hit the front wall on the fly, it is also considered a failure to return and results in loss of the rally.

Dead Ball Hinders

Generally any type of interference in play that is unavoidable results in a dead ball hinder. There is no penalty to either player, and the point is replayed. This type of hinder cancels any prior fault serve. That is, the server starts the point with two chances to make a legal serve. You may learn about avoidable hinders when you enter tournament or league play. Avoidable hinders are usually called only by referees. Here are the more common dead ball hinders.

Court Hinder

This occurs when the ball hits any part of the court that has been damaged and results in an irregular bounce. Such bounces can also occur from door cracks, light fixtures, and so on.

Hitting Opponent

When a legal return hits an opponent on the fly before it returns to the front wall, it is a hinder. The player hit should make the call and stop play.

Body Contact

Body contact or stopping to avoid body contact is a hinder if it interferes with a fair chance to play the ball. The person hindered should make the call. Body contact, particularly on the follow-through, is not necessarily a hinder.

Screen Ball

This was also described in the section on dead ball serves. If the ball rebounds so close to the player that the returner's view of the ball is obstructed, the returner should call a screen ball hinder.

Safety Holdup

Any time a player is afraid that her or his swing or the ball may strike the opponent, the player should call a hinder.

There are many other technical rules of racquetball, but the ones listed here will enable you to play the game and enjoy it. You don't have to memorize these rules, but read them enough to be familiar with them. You can always refer back to them if a question arises.

RACQUETBALL TODAY

Racquetball has become so popular that you probably have easy access to a court wherever you live or work. Most YMCAs have courts available, and practically all communities of 15,000 or more have private racquet clubs. The building boom has slowed as more courts have become available, but racquetball is firmly established as a popular recreational sport, with 8.5 million players.

The United States Olympic Committee has granted Group A membership to racquetball, making it the youngest sport ever to achieve that status. This means that racquetball will probably be an exhibition sport in the next Olympics. If that happens, racquetball may experience a new period of growth and could be added to the list of official Olympic sports in the future.

If you join a racquet club, you will find that tournaments and league play are sponsored by almost all organizations that have courts. Regional and national tournaments are also sponsored by the American Amateur Racquetball Association for those who wish to compete at a higher level. To receive further information, contact:

American Amateur Racquetball Association
815 N. Weber, Suite 101
Colorado Springs, CO 80903

Basic Equipment and Clothing

Clothing and equipment have changed considerably in recent years. Manufacturers have responded to the boom in racquetball with state-of-the-art equipment, so that the technology available is similar to that for tennis.

You need not have the latest and most expensive equipment to learn the game, however. To spend too much on equipment is foolish, because you may find out later that you prefer something else. To spend too little is often wasteful, also. Very cheap equipment will probably not be adequate or even last long enough for you to discover what type of equipment is best for you. Buy moderately priced equipment that appears to be well constructed. Many organizations furnish racquets and eye guards on a "check out" basis.

RACQUETS

You probably have a racquet at your disposal. It would be best to borrow one until you are sure you wish to pursue the game. You can also try several different kinds to see which you prefer. Racquets are made from several types of materials including wood, fiberglass, metal alloys, and graphite. The construction varies and affects the price. Prices vary from $15 to $200 and depend upon quality. A good-quality metal racquet costing about $25 will give several years of service. By that time you will know more about what racquet you will want next. Several different sizes and weights are available. The most important consideration for a beginner is the size of the grip. This will vary from 3-1/4 inches to 4-1/2 inches. The size is printed on or near the handle of many racquets. To check your racquet grip for size, wrap your fingers around the handle. Your two middle fingers should barely touch the base of your thumb (see Figure 2). The fit can vary slightly without affecting performance, but a grip that is too large or small will affect both power and control.

All racquets should have a thong (string or cord) attached to the handle. For safety

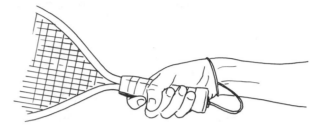

Figure 2 Proper grip (handle) size permits two middle fingers to touch base of thumb lightly.

reasons, the rules state that players must have this thong around the wrist during play.

RACQUETBALLS

Racquetballs are usually available at your local sporting goods store. They come in cans of two. They are usually under pressure to assure that they will be "fresh" and bounce correctly. Most are blue or black in color. If you purchase racquetballs, look for balls that are approved by the AARA.

SHOES

Beginners often don't realize the importance of good footwear. A good, solid shoe with a flat sole is essential. The action is fast and calls for quick movements in all directions. A shoe made for tennis, basketball, or racquetball can be purchased at most sporting goods stores or department stores. Do not try to play in jogging shoes—the high-wedge heel makes them unstable and unsuitable for racquetball. It is also important to have a good, heavy pair of socks to help prevent blisters and absorb moisture. Two pairs of socks can often minimize friction that causes blisters. If you wear two pairs, use lighter weight socks.

OTHER CLOTHING

The main consideration is that your clothes are comfortable and allow you to move freely. A standard pair of athletic shorts and a shirt will do. Some people wear sweatpants or other long pants to cover their legs in case the ball hits them in the back of the leg. There are no other requirements except that for tournaments you must wear light-colored clothes. Dark-colored clothes make it harder to see the ball when it passes your body.

EYE GUARDS

Eye guards are strongly recommended for racquetball play. Most of the serious injuries in the sport occur to the eye. Professionals wear them at all times. They are required for all players in all AARA-sanctioned tournaments. Don't be caught without them. Special eye guards are available that fit over prescription glasses. Or, special eye guards with prescrip-tion lenses can be made by your eye care specialist.

GLOVES

Gloves help prevent the racquet from slipping or turning in your hand. They come in several materials. Leather is traditional, but newer materials do not harden when they get wet from perspiration.

OTHER ACCESSORIES

Headbands and wristbands help protect from perspiration. Sweat in your eyes or on your hand could disturb your concentration.

Safety and Etiquette for Success

Racquetball is played in a small, enclosed space. With two or more people moving quickly and swinging racquets, safety and etiquette are important considerations. A safe and pleasant environment makes learning and playing much more enjoyable. Some simple rules will create that environment.

SAFETY

There are several safe practices one should observe during play.

1. Figure 3 shows a person wearing protective eye wear. As stated before, this is a necessity. Most of the serious injuries in racquetball are to the eyes. A hard-hit racquetball can travel over 100 miles per hour.

Figure 3 Person wearing safety glasses.

2. In addition to wearing eye guards, do not look back at your opponent if she or he is making a shot from behind you. Keep your eyes fixed on the front wall. This will also make you a better player, as you will be better able to react to the ball.
3. Figure 4 illustrates use of the thong that should be attached to all racquets. It is a rule of racquetball that the racquet must be secured to the wrist. To play otherwise is a loss of the point as well as a foolish safety violation.
4. Another safe practice is to not swing at the ball if there is a danger that your rac-

Figure 4 String (thong) to secure racquet to wrist.

quet or the ball will strike your opponent. There is no penalty to either player. This situation is called a hinder and results in a replay of the point. These hinders will become less frequent as beginning players gain experience in their movement patterns. Do not hesitate to call this type of hinder. Your opponent will appreciate it.
5. Another type of hinder occurs when players collide or get in each other's way while moving into position. Assuming the interference was not intentional, the person who was ''hindered'' should announce it, and the point should be replayed with no penalty to either player. Hinders are unique to racquetball and illustrate a combination of safety and etiquette concerns. There are other types of hinders that are not related to safety. Review the rules to make sure that you understand the concept of hinders.

ETIQUETTE

Racquetball is usually played without a referee. This makes sportsmanship and etiquette very important and integral to the game. It also adds greatly to the enjoyment of the game. The person who practices good sportsmanship will always be able to find someone with whom to enjoy friendly competition. Here are some specific items of etiquette you should practice while playing racquetball:

1. Call out the score (yours first) when serving. This will eliminate any confusion and arguments throughout the game.
2. Wait until the receiver is ready before serving.
3. Refrain from talking during play. It is acceptable to congratulate your opponent on a good shot while the ball is dead. To talk while your opponent is making a shot is illegal as well as unethical. Any other deliberate distractions by your opponent are equally illegal.
4. Control your temper. No one wants to play with someone who can't. Control the temptation to hit the ball in disgust after the point is over. Your opponent will have relaxed and is vulnerable at this time.
5. Be fair on your calls. Give the benefit of the doubt to your opponent. Talk it over. If a decision is not easily reached, replay the point. The reputation for fair play spreads as fast as one for being a "poor sport."
6. Make an effort to give your opponent a fair chance to play the ball. Don't obstruct his or her view or move so close to your opponent that you interfere with his or her swing or concentration.
7. If you must talk to yourself between points, keep it low and positive. Derogatory remarks about your ability or your excuse for not making a shot are really an insult to your opponent. In no case will they help you to play better.
8. Thank your opponent for a match. Congratulate the opponent if she or he won. Keep any excuses for poor play to yourself. No one else wants to hear them, especially not a person who has just defeated you.

Warming Up for Success

The warm-up is often neglected by people in a hurry, who arrive late and don't want to waste any time before getting into the activity. Racquetball is no exception. What these people don't realize is that they may be hindering their performance in addition to risking serious and even permanent injury.

WHY IS THE WARM-UP IMPORTANT?

Regardless of why you play or the level at which you play, a proper warm-up is essential. A good warm-up enables you to participate with less discomfort, helps prevent injuries, and generally lets you enjoy the activity more. Specifically, you need to get your blood flowing to supply energy to the muscles you are asking to do the work. Increasing the temperature of your body allows this to happen more efficiently. Increased temperature also allows muscles, tendons, and ligaments to operate with less chance of tearing.

WARM-UP PROCEDURE

All warm-ups should be started slowly and gently. Then gradually increase the intensity so your body can easily adjust to the increased demands. When extended for 5 to 10 minutes, the warm-up should prepare your body for vigorous activity.

There are three parts to your racquetball warm-up. You must warm up your cardiovascular system and then the specific muscles involved in the activity. Finally, you should stretch the muscles and joints in your body to help avoid injuries.

Warm-Up of the Cardiovascular System

Your heart, lungs, and blood vessels need to be properly warmed up first. By increasing your heart rate and temperature, you are preparing your system to respond to increased demands during strenuous activity. There are several ways to accomplish this. One is by warming up with specific shots, as described later. If you continue with this activity, you will begin to perspire, and your heart rate will increase. Moderate sweating is a good indicator that your cardiovascular system is warmed up. This should take from 5 to 10 minutes but could be continued longer if desired. Other ways to achieve this part of your warm-up are by jogging, doing jumping jacks, or simply jumping up and down. Regardless of the method, start slowly and gradually increase the pace or rate. And above all, don't start playing a game until you have accomplished a proper warm-up.

Warm-Up of Specific Muscles— Hitting

Probably the most important thing to remember here is to start slow and increase your intensity and effort. Start by gently making the kinds of movements you make during play. Swing your racquet without hitting a ball. Rotate your arms, shoulders, and hips as you go through all your hitting motions. Next go through your entire array of shots, hitting the ball easy at first. Then gradually increase the power. As you learn the different shots of racquetball, you should incorporate them into this warm-up. Many of the drills in this book make excellent warm-ups. Many players suffer sore shoulders and elbows because they fail to warm up gradually. Spending the proper amount of time in warm-up can prevent most of these injuries.

Stretching

The most important point to remember here is *do not bounce*! Put an easy stretch on your muscle or joint and then just hold it for 5 to 10 seconds. Concentrate on the muscle being stretched and try to make it relax. After 5 to 10 seconds you may be able to stretch it a little further, but remember to keep it a static stretch.

Reach-Out Arm Stretch

Interlace your fingers out in front of you at shoulder height. Turn your palms outward as you extend your arms forward to feel a stretch in your shoulders, middle of upper back, arms, hands, fingers, and wrists. Hold an easy stretch for 15 seconds, then relax and repeat.

Reach-Up Arm Stretch

Interlace your fingers above your head. Now, with your palms facing upward, push your arms slightly back and up. Feel the stretch in your arms, shoulders, and upper back. Hold the stretch for 15 seconds. Don't hold your breath.

Arm and Shoulder Stretch

With your legs under you, reach forward and grab the end of a carpet or mat. If you can't grab on to something, just pull back with both arms straight while you press down slightly with your palms (see Figure a). You can also do this stretch one arm at a time (see Figure b). Pulling with just one arm provides more control and isolates the stretch on either side. Hold for 15 seconds. Don't strain. Be relaxed.

a

b

Forearm and Wrist Stretch

Start on all fours. Support yourself on your hands and knees. Your thumbs should be pointed to the outside with your fingers pointed toward your knees. Keep your palms flat as you lean back to stretch the front part of your forearms. Hold an easy stretch for 20 seconds. Relax, then stretch again.

Deltoid and Triceps Stretch

Clasp and gently pull your elbow behind your head. Keep your head and neck erect. Hold an easy stretch for 10 seconds for each arm, 20 seconds total.

Shoulder Socket Stretch

This shoulder stretch can be done in two parts. Start with your fingers interlaced behind your back. For the first stretch, slowly turn your elbows inward while straightening your arms (see Figure a). If that is fairly easy, then lift your arms up behind you until you feel a stretch in your arms, shoulders, or chest (see Figure b). Hold an easy stretch for 15 to 20 seconds. Keep your chest out and chin in.

Inner Thigh Stretch

While in a seated position, pull the soles of your feet together (see Figure a). With your hands clasped around your feet, slowly pull yourself forward until you feel a stretch in the groin area (see Figure b). Do not bounce your knees up and down. Hold an easy stretch for 15 seconds. Slowly increase the stretch as you feel yourself relax. Hold the developmental stretch for 15 seconds.

 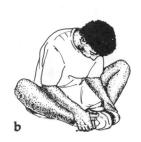

Iliopsoas and Quadriceps Stretch

From a position commonly called the "mountain climber," move one foot forward until the knee of the forward leg is directly over your ankle. Your other knee should be resting on the floor. Now, without changing the position of the knee on the floor or the forward foot, lower the front of your hip downward to create an easy stretch. Hold for 30 seconds. You should feel this stretch in the front of the hip and possibly in the hamstrings and groin.

Straddle Stretch (Hamstring)

Sit on the floor with your legs straight. Move your feet as far apart as possible without straining. Keep your feet upright and relaxed. Now slowly lean straight forward until you feel a stretch on the inside of your legs. Keep your hips forward. Hold an easy stretch for 20 seconds (see Figure a). Sit up straight.

Stretch your left hamstring and back by bending at the waist toward the foot of your left leg. Keep your head up (look at your foot) as you feel a good but controlled stretch. Hold for 20 seconds (see Figure b). Repeat with the other leg for 20 seconds.

flat. Be sure to keep the heel of the straight leg on the ground, with your toes pointed straight ahead or slightly turned in as you hold the stretch. Hold an easy stretch for 30 seconds. Don't bounce. Stretch your other leg the same way.

b

Ankle Rotation

In a seated position, grasp your lower leg with one hand and your foot with the other hand. Rotate your ankle clockwise and counterclockwise through a complete range of motion with your hand. Rotary motion of the ankle helps to gently stretch out tight ligaments. Repeat 10 to 20 times in each direction.

Soleus Stretch

To create a stretch for the soleus muscle and Achilles tendon, assume the same starting position as for the calf stretch, only closer to the wall and use your back (right) toe for balance. Lower your hips downward as you slightly bend your knee. Be sure to keep your back flat. Your front foot should be slightly toed-in or straight ahead during the stretch. Keep your heel down. This stretch is good for developing ankle flexibility. Hold this stretch for 25 seconds. The Achilles tendon area needs only a slight feeling of stretch.

Calf Stretch

To stretch your calf, stand about 2 or 3 feet from the wall. Lean on the wall with your forearms, with your head near your hands and your back straight. Bend one leg and place your foot on the ground in front of you, with the other leg straight behind. Slowly move your hips forward, keeping your lower back

Spinal Twist

The spinal twist is good for the upper back, lower back, sides of the hips, and rib cage. It will increase your ability to turn to the side or look behind you without having to turn your entire body.

Sit with your right leg straight. Bend your left leg, cross your left foot over and rest it on the outside of your right knee. Then bend your right elbow and rest it on the outside of your upper left thigh, just above the knee. During the stretch use the elbow to keep this leg stationary with controlled pressure to the inside.

Now with your left hand palm down on the floor behind you and your left arm straight, slowly turn your head to look over your left shoulder, and at the same time rotate your upper body toward your left hand and arm. As you turn your upper body, think of turning your hips in the same direction (though your hips won't move, because your right elbow is keeping the left leg stationary). This should give you a stretch in your lower back and the side of your hip. Hold for 15 seconds. Do both sides. Don't hold your breath; breathe easily.

COOL-DOWN

After playing or practicing, be sure to take 5 to 10 minutes to return your body to normal. You must continue your movement to redistribute the blood in your system, slow your pulse rate, and lower your body temperature.

After a match, walk around for 5 to 10 minutes until your pulse returns to within 40 beats of normal. That is, if your normal heart rate is 70, continue your cool-down until your pulse rate is 110 or lower.

Repeat any or all of the stretches done at the outset. Be sure to stretch the lower back and achilles tendon if you don't do any others; walking will help stretch the quadriceps.

Step 1 The Grips—Forehand, Backhand, Continental

This step introduces you to the various ways to grip the racquet. Often there are no right or wrong ways to do things, as long as you get the results you want. However, most successful players use common fundamentals. Try these widely accepted grips to achieve a higher degree of initial success. As you develop your skill, you may wish to experiment with different fundamentals and techniques.

WHY IS THE GRIP IMPORTANT?

How you grip the racquet is the most basic of all the skills and techniques in racquetball. The grip affects the quality and direction of your shots as you swing the racquet. Therefore, it is crucial that you develop and maintain the grip that is best for you. There are two basic systems: the Eastern forehand and backhand, and the Continental. The Eastern grips are preferred by most experienced players. The advantage is in giving you better control of the direction of the ball, especially on backhand shots. The disadvantage is that you must remember to switch between forehand and backhand grips during play. Your teacher or friend can help you with this decision. Start with one system, and stick with it until you have played for several weeks. Then experiment with the other system if you wish.

HOW TO GRIP THE RACQUET

Most racquet handles have eight edges, or ''bevels'' (see Figure 1.1; if your racquet is round, just use the same basic locations as a guide). Notice that reference is made to the top back corner bevel that is on the opposite side of the direction of the stroke. The back side changes depending upon whether you are hitting a forehand or backhand shot. Figure 1.2 shows the main contact points on the palm side of your hand that you will use to grip the racquet; check them as you assume

your grip. Figure 1.3, illustrates the V formed by the thumb and forefinger. You will use this V as a key checkpoint for all the grips.

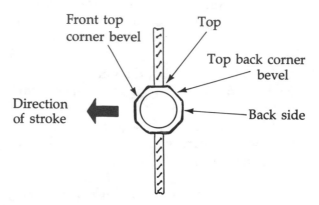

Figure 1.1 Parts of a racquet handle from a right-handed player's point-of-view.

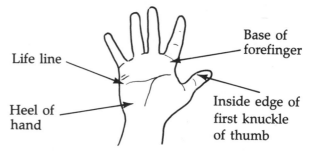

Figure 1.2 Main palm contacts used to grip the racquet.

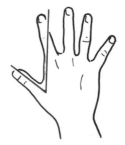

Figure 1.3 The ''V'' formed by your thumb and forefinger.

Eastern Forehand Grip

To grip the racquet for a forehand stroke with the Eastern grip, grasp the handle so that the V formed by your thumb and forefinger is centered on the top back corner bevel. If you are right-handed, your wrist is slightly to the right of the handle (see Figure 1.4a); if you are left handed, your wrist is slightly to the left. Most racquet grips are made of leather, wrapped in a diagonal pattern on the handle. Your fingers should be at approximately the same angle as the wrapping (see Figure 1.4b). If there is no wrapping, make sure your fingers are at an angle to the length of the handle. Now, using the Keys to Success in Figure 1.5, a-d, try the Eastern forehand grip.

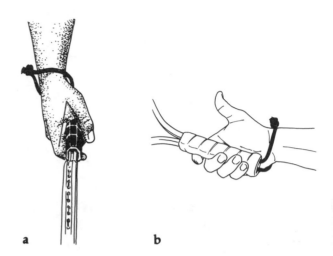

a   **b**

Figure 1.4 Eastern forehand grip from two different angles.

Figure 1.5 Keys to Success: Eastern Forehand Grip

**Preparation
Phase**

1. Grasp top edge of racquet head with non-racquet hand ____
2. Hold racquet so face is perpendicular to floor ____
3. Place palm of outstretched hand against strings ____

a

Execution
Phase

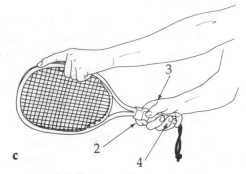

1. Slide racquet hand down strings toward handle ____
2. Close fingers around grip as if shaking hands ____

3. V of hand is on top back corner bevel ____
4. Ends of fingers lightly touching hand ____

Self-Check
Phase

1. Turn hand over—palm up ____
2. Open thumb—still holding racquet ____
3. Fingers holding racquet ____
4. "Life line" visible on thumb side of palm (see Figure 1.2) ____
5. Fingers diagonally across handle ____
6. Ends of fingers on flat side ____
7. Racquet handle diagonally across palm ____
8. Heel of hand and base of forefinger as main contact points ____
9. Thong around wrist ____

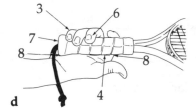

Eastern Backhand Grip

To assume the Eastern backhand grip simply grasp the racquet in the Eastern forehand grip and rotate your hand one quarter of a turn backward from the direction of the stroke. Now the V formed by your thumb and forefinger should be centered on the top back corner bevel (the side away from the direction of the stroke). The side of your thumb should rest against the lower back corner bevel. The heel of your hand should be on the top bevel and the base of your forefinger on the top front corner bevel (see Figure 1.6). The Keys to Success in Figure 1.7, a-d, show the Eastern backhand grip.

Figure 1.6 Eastern backhand grip.

Figure 1.7 Keys to Success: Eastern Backhand Grip

Preparation Phase

1. Assume Eastern forehand grip ____

Execution Phase

1. With other hand hold racquet ____
2. Rotate racquet hand one quarter turn back ____
3. V on top back corner bevel ____
4. Side of thumb against back side ____

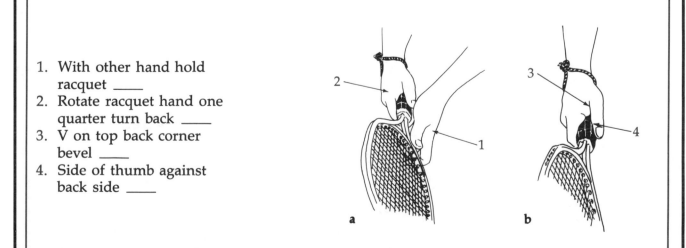

**Self-Check
Phase**

1. Turn hand over—palm up ____
2. Open hand—retain racquet ____
3. Fingers gripping racquet ____
4. More of life line visible ____
5. Ends of fingers on lower back corner bevel ____
6. Heel of hand on top bevel ____
7. Base of forefinger on top front corner bevel ____
8. Thong around wrist ____

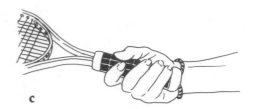

c

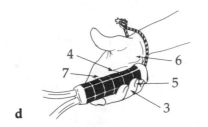

d

Continental Grip

The Continental grip, which is the same for forehand and backhand strokes, is often used by beginners and lower level players. Its advantage is that no time is required to change grips during a rally. This allows beginners to concentrate on other areas of the game during play. The disadvantage is that the player must rotate the arm or change body position to change the face of the racquet for the backhand stroke. This causes slight difficulties in both power and control.

To get the feel of the Continental grip, ro-tate your hand slightly back from the Eastern forehand grip, about half the distance to the Eastern backhand grip. The V of the hand should be on the top bevel. Two factors can help you decide which grip to try first. Have you played other racquet sports, like tennis or badminton? If so, you may want to try the Eastern grips. If not, you may want to start with the Continental grip. The other factor is how well you can think during game action. If you can think about several things at a time, use the Eastern grips. If not, start with the Continental grip, as shown in Figure 1.8.

Figure 1.8 Keys to Success: Continental Grip

**Preparation
Phase**

1. Assume Eastern forehand grip ____

**Execution
Phase**

1. Rotate your racquet
   hand slightly back ____
2. V on top bevel ____
3. Side of thumb against
   back side ____

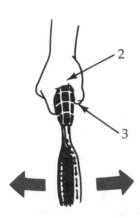

IMPORTANT GRIP CONSIDERATIONS

Some of these grip considerations have been briefly mentioned. They are included here to give you a complete summary of important basics to developing a better grip. A good grip does not guarantee success at racquetball—it's only the start. But a poor grip will almost guarantee a lack of success.

Size

To check the size of your racquet, grip it; your middle fingers should just lightly touch the base of your thumb. You can play with a grip size that is too large or too small, but your control will be affected. Players who are accustomed to a tennis racquet usually have to adjust to the feeling that the racquetball handle is too small. This smaller handle size is necessary to get the proper wrist action that is required in racquetball but taboo in tennis.

Tension

As you start your swing, your grip tightens so you have a firm grip at impact. Between hits, however, you should relax your grip. This is important for two reasons. First, your fingers and hand will get extremely tired if you don't, limiting your racquet control and power as the game or match continues. Second, you may need to change to a forehand or backhand grip. This is impossible to do with a tight grip.

Relaxing your grip should become a natural habit as you play more.

Control

You can "choke up" on the racquet by moving your hand up toward the head. This may reduce your power, but the resulting gain of control is well worth it. As you develop better control, you can move down the handle until your hand is even with the end, or "butt," of the handle. Some experienced players choke up their grip at critical points in a game to increase control.

Wrist Extension

As mentioned before, your fingers should rest diagonally on the grip. When you open your hand you should be able to retain control of the racquet and also see your life line in the palm of your hand. Figure 1.9 shows how the wrist can be extended with the proper grip, greatly extending the reach and allowing your wrist to "cock" and "uncock" (or release) during your swing to give you greater power.

Figure 1.9 Proper grip and wrist extension.

Detecting Errors in the Grip

Your grip greatly affects the quality of your shot. Some shots are impossible with a poor grip. If you find yourself having problems controlling the ball, the first thing to check is your grip. Even experienced players go back and review the grip when they are trying to improve or regain their game.

ERROR 🚫

CORRECTION

ERROR	CORRECTION
1. Forehand lacks power.	1. Review your grip (see Drills 2, 3, and 7).
2. Forehand seems OK, but backhand stroke is restricted.	2. Remember to change grip to backhand or Continental. Use opposite hand to help. Side of thumb should rest against handle. Make sure you are not using the "frying pan" grip (see Drill 1).
3. Wrist feels stiff or restricted during swing.	3. Handle should not be held too "deep" in the palm of your hand (perpendicular to handle). Grip it with your fingers (see Drill 5).
4. Hand and fingers tire easily.	4. Relax grip between strokes. Build strength by squeezing a racquetball, towel, or other object.

Grip Drills

All the following drills are important for getting the proper feel of the grip. They are valuable to experienced players as a review and to beginners to insure a proper foundation. To reinforce the feel of the grip, swing the racquet each time without a ball. Concentrate on the feel as you are swinging, and internalize the proper feeling.

1. Frying Pan

Lay the racquet flat on the floor. Pick the racquet up by the handle. Notice that the V between the thumb and forefinger is on the large flat side of the handle. This is an incorrect grip. Swing the racquet at an imaginary ball and remember how it looks and feels.

Success Goal = 10 incorrect grips and swings

Your Score = (#) _____ incorrect grips and swings

2. "Shake Hands"

Take turns with a partner. Hold the racquet face perpendicular to the floor. Have your partner grab the handle with the "shake hands" grip. The partner's wrist will be slightly to the backside of the grip, and the V formed by the thumb and forefinger will be on the top back bevel. Have your partner swing the racquet while you check her or his grip. Then switch roles and repeat. Review the Eastern Forehand Grip Keys to Success in Figure 1.5.

Success Goal = 10 correct "shake hands" grips and swings with the racquet

Your Score = (#) _____ correct grips and swings

3. Backhand Grip

Assume the forehand grip. Rotate your racquet hand one quarter turn backward. The V should be on the top back corner bevel (opposite the direction of the stroke). Swing the racquet. Partners should check grips. Review the Eastern Backhand Grip Keys to Success in Figure 1.7.

Success Goal = 10 correct backhand grips and swings

Your Score = (#) _____ correct backhand grips and swings

4. Change Grips

With or without a partner, assume the forehand grip. Change grips back and forth two or three times without looking. Stop and then check to see if you have proper grip.

Success Goal = 10 correct grips

Your Score = (#) _____ correct grips

5. Finger Control

With a partner, assume the forehand grip. Turn your hand so your palm is up. Open your hand partly to show your partner the life line in the palm of your hand while still retaining control of the racquet in your fingers. The fingers should be at an angle across the handle. Close your hand. Change to a backhand grip and repeat.

Success Goal = 10 grips with correct finger position

Your Score = (#) _____ grips with correct finger position

6. *Extended Wrist*

Assume a forehand grip with finger control. Straighten your arm and point your racquet toward a spot on the wall. If you have a proper grip and finger control, the racquet handle should look like an extension of your arm. At the wrist, there should be a very slight angle (about 20 degrees) between the hand and lower arm. Partners should check this from the side. Exchange places and repeat the drill.

Success Goal = 10 correct wrist positions

Your Score = (#) _____ correct wrist positions

7. *Continental Grip*

Assume a forehand grip. Rotate your hand backward until the V is halfway between the forehand and the backhand grip (on the top bevel). Your partner should check its position. Review the Continental Grip Keys to Success in Figure 1.8. Swing the racquet to get the feel of this grip. Your partner then repeats the drill.

Success Goal = 10 correct Continental grips and swings

Your Score = (#) _____ correct Continental grips and swings

Grip
Keys to Success Checklist

Now that you have tried the different grips, choose either the Eastern system or the Continental. Use it for a week or two to get the feel of it. Change to the other system if you are having trouble controlling the ball at that time. Before you are ready to work on your control of the ball with your racquet, ask your teacher or another trained observer to evaluate your selected grip using the proper Keys to Success checklists (see either Figures 1.5 and 1.7, or 1.8). Review this step on the grip often if you have not played much racquetball.

Step 2 **Developing Control of the Ball**

Experienced players know that control is the "name of the game." Power is only important when a player advances to a higher level of skill. Even then, power is still secondary to control. Why, then, do most beginners hit the ball as hard as they can without much thought to direction? Human nature is one possible explanation. A need to let out one's aggressions might be another reason. Whatever the case, you must sooner or later develop good control of the ball to progress as a player. It is much easier to start developing that control at the outset.

If you have not played many racquet sports, the racquet may feel strange to you. The activities in this step will help you feel more comfortable with a racquet in your hand. They are also designed to help you develop better hand–eye coordination as well. Hand–eye coordination varies greatly with individuals, so if it doesn't come easily for you, have patience. It can be improved with practice, and you can still have fun while improving.

WHY IS CONTROL OF THE BALL IMPORTANT?

In all ball sports, the ability to control the ball is of crucial importance. You will be playing against someone else in a small space, so you have little room for error on each shot. Careless or inaccurate shots will soon get you in trouble. On the other hand, the ability to control the ball allows you to control the game and your opponent. A skilled older player can easily defeat a young, physically fit player who has not mastered the art of controlling the ball. When you meet a player who wants to use power and gives little thought to control, you will have an advantage if you keep your goals in mind and fight power with control.

RACQUET ANGLE AND DIRECTION OF THE BALL

The angle of the racquet face is what determines the direction the ball travels. The angle of the face is influenced by two factors: position of the ball at contact relative to the body, and wrist action. The angle can vary in two planes. Looking from the top, the face can be open, square, or closed in relation to the body and the front wall (see Figure 2.1). The ball will rebound perpendicular to the face, so an open face will cause the ball to go to the right (for a right-handed player). A square face will result in the ball traveling straight forward to the wall and straight back. A closed face

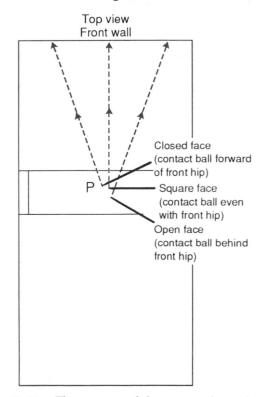

Figure 2.1 The position of the racquet face relative to ball contact and the front wall determines the direction the ball travels.

causes the ball to go to the left. The angle of the racquet face in this plane is affected by where the ball is contacted in relation to the body. When the ball is contacted out in front of the body (nearer the front wall), the racquet face closes, causing the ball to go to the left (see Figure 2.2). Contacting the ball even with

Figure 2.2 A closed face causes the ball to go left.

the front hip (approximately) causes a square face and resulting ball direction straight forward (see Figure 2.3). Contacting the ball behind the front hip (relative to the front wall) results in an open face and ball direction to the right (see Figure 2.4).

Figure 2.3 A square face causes the ball to go straight.

Viewed from the side, the racquet face can also vary from open to square to closed (see Figure 2.5, a through c). As you can see, an open face results in the ball going upward toward the ceiling, and a closed face directs the ball toward the floor. Rotation of the arm and wrist will control the racquet angle in this plane.

Figure 2.4 An open face sends the ball right.

The height of the ball also affects the angle of the racquet. As you contact the ball low or high, your swing changes from a sidearm swing to an underhand or an overhead swing. This results in a combination of racquet angles. The number of combinations is endless, but don't let that confuse you. Think about the basic angles and directions; let your subconscious make the adjustments.

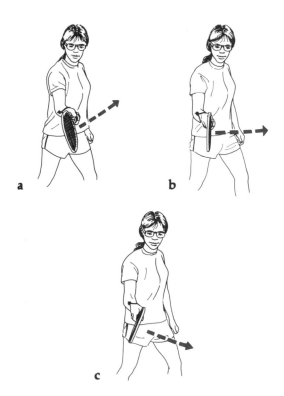

Figure 2.5 A side view of the wrist's effect on the racquet face, causing the ball to go upward (open face; a), straight (square face; b), or toward the floor (closed face; c).

Racquet Control Drills

These drills will help you develop ball control. In the first three drills, the grip isn't so important, because the direction of the ball is different from what it would be during a game. Focus on watching the ball and developing hand–eye coordination. The other drills develop angles you will encounter in a game. Therefore, make sure you have decided upon a grip (Eastern or Continental) and use the proper grip while practicing Drills 4 and 5.

1. Dribble Bounce

Stand on any flat surface. Assume the forehand, Continental, or frying-pan grip. Bounce the ball on the floor with the racquet within a small area. To add more of a challenge, try this drill keeping your left foot in the same place. Finally, try this drill walking or running around the court or on any designated path.

Success Goals = 25 consecutive bounces in each of 3 ways: within a small area; keeping left foot in place; and either walking or running

Your Scores =

    a. (#) ____ consecutive bounces within a small area

    b. (#) ____ consecutive bounces keeping left foot in place

    c. (#) ____ consecutive bounces while walking or running

2. Air Dribble

Stand in any open area. Keep the ball in the air with consecutive hits off your racquet. Hit the ball softly with control. It should bounce only 2 to 4 feet above the racquet. Now try air dribbles keeping your left foot in one place. Next try air dribbles walking or running. Finally, try hitting the ball with alternate sides of racquet face while standing in one place.

Success Goals = 25 consecutive air dribbles in each of 4 ways: any way; with left foot fixed; while walking or running; and using alternate sides of racquet

Your Scores =

a. (#) _____ consecutive air dribbles

b. (#) _____ consecutive air dribbles with left foot fixed

c. (#) _____ consecutive air dribbles while walking or running

d. (#) _____ consecutive air dribbles using alternate sides of racquet

3. *The Edge*

Bounce the ball on the ground using only the edge of the racquet. Obviously, you wouldn't try this during a game, but it will train you to watch the ball closely. If you really want a challenge, try to bounce the ball in the air using only the edge of the racquet.

Success Goals = 10 consecutive bounces in two ways: on the floor; and in the air

Your Scores =

a. (#) _____ consecutive bounces on the floor

b. (#) _____ consecutive bounces in the air

4. *Wall Rally*

Stand 4 to 5 feet from any straight wall. Tap the ball softly against the wall. Play it on one bounce and return it to the wall. Keep it in play. Proper grip is important in this drill. Use your forehand grip first. Then try it using your backhand grip. Next try alternating your forehand and backhand strokes. (Remember to change grips.) Finally, you can play the ball on the fly (volley) and keep it in the air.

Success Goals = 25 consecutive returns in each of 4 ways with proper grip: with forehand; with backhand; alternate forehand and backhand; and with volley

Your Scores =

a. (#) _____ consecutive returns using proper forehand stroke

b. (#) _____ consecutive returns using proper backhand stroke

c. (#) _____ consecutive returns alternating proper forehand and backhand strokes

d. (#) _____ consecutive returns using volley

5. *Angle Control*

Standing in the service area near the center, drop the ball and stroke it to a partner standing in the service area near the left wall. Face the right wall and use your forehand. You will have to drop the ball in front of your body so the racquet face is closed as it contacts the ball. Hit the ball softly with control so your partner can catch it after one bounce. The important thing is to develop control and learn where to position yourself to direct the ball to your left.

Ask your partner to move to the right side wall, and repeat this drill. Still using your forehand grip, contact the ball nearer your rear hip so your racquet face is open upon contact. Remember to hit the ball softly with control.

Next, repeat both of these drills using your backhand grip and dropping the ball on the backhand side of your body. Try to visualize the path the ball must take to reach your partner before you hit each shot. Also visualize the spot on the front wall that will give your shot the proper angle to reach your partner.

Success Goals = 10 shots within 4 to 5 feet of partner's position in each of 4 ways: to left, then right using forehand; and to left, then right using backhand

Your Scores =

    a. (#) _____ shots to left using forehand

    b. (#) _____ shots to right using forehand

    c. (#) _____ shots to left using backhand

    d. (#) _____ shots to right using backhand

Step 3 Basic Strokes— Forehand and Backhand

The two strokes used most often in racquetball are the forehand and backhand. A forehand stroke is used when the ball comes to the side of your body on which you hold the racquet. You will use it more than any other stroke. The backhand stroke is used when the ball comes to the other side of your body (the nonracquet side). The backhand stroke is usually more difficult to master, but with practice all players can improve. Good players usually will take advantage of an opponent who has a weak backhand by hitting to his or her backhand often.

WHY ARE THE FOREHAND AND BACKHAND STROKES IMPORTANT?

The forehand and backhand are the foundation of all the strokes used in racquetball. You will hit 75 percent of your shots with these strokes, and the rest of your shots will be modifications of these strokes. The backhand is especially important because it can be a glaring weakness if you do not develop it to an adequate level. Better players have strong backhands and can use them to win points and end rallies as well as to defend themselves. The ready position is a transition position to assume between strokes.

THE READY POSITION

The ready position is similar to the ready position in many sports. Your weight is evenly balanced on both feet. Your shoulders and hips are square to the front wall. Your head is up and your eyes are focused straight ahead on the front wall. Hold your racquet in front of you. Your nonracquet hand can be on the racquet, ready to help you change your grip.

This is the position you want to assume after every shot just prior to your movement. If you move to the location you desire and the ball has not been returned, maintain this ready position so you can move quickly to a new lo-

cation if necessary. Figure 3.1 illustrates this ready position.

Figure 3.1   Ready position.

HOW TO EXECUTE THE FOREHAND

You have already learned the forehand grip. Assume this grip, making sure your wrist is slightly to the right of the top of the handle (a left-hander's wrist would be slightly to the left). As soon as you know the ball is coming to the forehand side, move quickly to the general area where you expect to make the shot. Estimate the speed and path of the ball and move to meet it. Do not chase it. While you are moving, you should begin your backswing. Don't forget to keep your eyes focused on the ball as you are moving. It is important to get into position early enough to allow enough time for adjustments for spin, velocity, and positioning mistakes. If the racquet is already back in position, you have more time to make a smooth, unhurried stroke. As you start your backswing, the racquet head moves downward and then loops back to point up toward the ceiling behind you. Your wrist should be cocked so your thumb points toward the ceiling.

As the ball comes to your forehand side, make your final adjustment to the ball so that it is even with or near your front hip. The actual position will depend on the angle at which you wish to return the ball, as was discussed in Step 2. Most of your weight should be on your rear foot, with that foot pointing to the side wall. Your front foot should point toward the front corner. Your shoulders and hips should be rotated slightly backward so that you are facing the side wall with your chest and "belt buckle."

As you start your forward swing, transfer your weight from the back foot to the front. As you hit, make sure that your weight moves forward. You may want to take a small step with your front foot to start this transfer.

This weight transfer is one of the most important parts of the stroke. Without it, you will be swinging entirely with your arm. This can make your arm very tired over the length of a game or match. It also will produce shots that lack power. Finally, shots hit without a good weight transfer tend to open the racquet face upward. This makes the shots hit the front wall higher than you are aiming, which in turn makes it easier for your opponent to return your shot. One way to check for proper weight transfer is to notice the position of the shoulder closest to the front wall. If it is about even with the other shoulder or is lower, your weight is forward. If it is higher or pointing upward, your weight is still on your rear foot.

As your weight transfers, your shoulders and hips should start rotating forward so that at the moment of contact they are approximately square to the front corner. You can also think of your front shoulder as pointing to "the net" (front wall) as in tennis. Your wrist uncocks (releases) so that the racquet is a straight extension of your arm and your thumb points down and forward toward the ball. The face of the racquet is now perpendicular to the intended line of flight of the ball and your arm is fully extended. Your arm should not be stiff but needs to be straight to give you a longer radius for your swing, so you develop good racquet-head speed. This speed will help you develop power so the ball travels faster. Try to see the ball hit the strings—even though this is not actually possible, it will help you stay focused on the ball during the shot, and this will keep you from pulling your head out early to anticipate where the ball is going.

Your fingers should grip the racquet firmly, but not so tightly that you can't get good wrist action. Usually you tighten your grip instinctively as you start your swing. You should practice consciously relaxing your grip between swings. If you don't, your fingers will get tired, losing both control and power. Don't forget to choke up (shorten) your grip when your hand gets tired or you want more control.

After you hit the ball, let the racquet follow the ball until it naturally starts across your body. As it does, your wrist will recock and your thumb will point up and behind you again. Your weight should be on your front foot, and your rear foot should come forward to a point approximately parallel to it. This enables you to stop your forward momentum and regain your balance. Your shoulders and hips will continue rotating forward until they are approximately parallel to the front wall. You should now be in the ready position and anticipating your next shot.

Every time you hit your forehand, the body action should be about the same (see Figure 3.2, a-f). As you get better, you will want to develop the ability to hit the ball lower on the front wall. To do this, wait for the ball to drop lower before swinging. This will require you to bend your knees or alter your swing path slightly. Better players learn to bend more and keep their stroke on a sidearm plane.

HOW TO EXECUTE THE BACKHAND

As you learned in Step 1, you can use the Eastern or Continental grip for the backhand stroke. Remember that the wrist should be on top and slightly to the back of the handle with the V on the top back bevel for the Eastern grip. The inside edge of the thumb should rest against the back flat part of the handle. Some beginners want to brace the thumb against the handle by having the bottom pad of the thumb contacting the handle. This should not be done, because it will severely restrict the wrist action necessary for a good backhand stroke. Keep the inside edge of the thumb against the handle.

As with all shots, determine where the ball is going to be and then go to meet it—don't chase it, because you will never catch it. Try to get there early to gain your balance and get ready for the shot. Start your backswing as you are moving into position. Take the racquet back with a down-and-back-up movement. Your eyes should be focused on the ball. At the top of your backswing, cock your wrist—thumb pointing upward. Keep or take your weight to your rear foot. As you take your racquet back, your hips and shoulders turn to face the rear corner. At this time you should be making your final adjustments so the ball will be in the correct position.

As you start your forward swing, push off your rear foot to start your weight moving forward. Start turning your hips and shoulders as you push off and bring your racquet forward. Hold your wrist cocked until you contact the ball, then let your wrist release so you give extra speed to the racquet head. You will have to practice this technique many times until you get the feel of the "snap" that gives power to the ball. Obviously you must focus on the ball carefully, to hit it properly.

As you release or snap your wrist, be sure to continue a full arm swing toward your target on the front wall. When your arm fully extends, it should move across your body to help pull your body around square to the front wall (see Figure 3.2, g-l). Your back foot comes around to a spot approximately even with your front foot. Regain your balance quickly and be ready to move to your next shot.

Figure 3.2 Keys to Success: The Basic Strokes

Preparation Phase

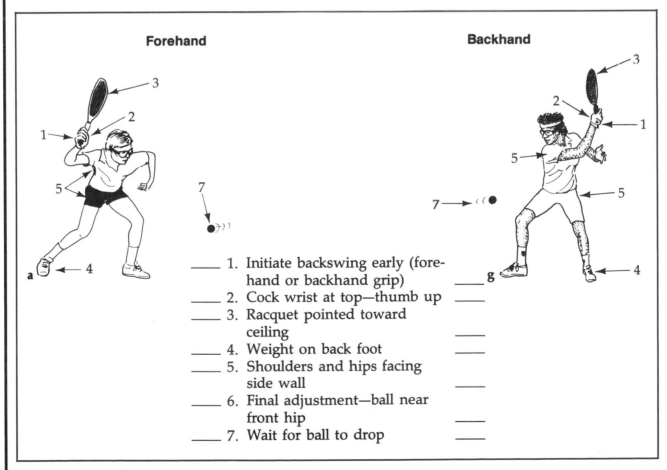

Forehand

Backhand

_____ 1. Initiate backswing early (forehand or backhand grip) _____

_____ 2. Cock wrist at top—thumb up _____

_____ 3. Racquet pointed toward ceiling _____

_____ 4. Weight on back foot _____

_____ 5. Shoulders and hips facing side wall _____

_____ 6. Final adjustment—ball near front hip _____

_____ 7. Wait for ball to drop _____

Execution Phase

Forehand

b

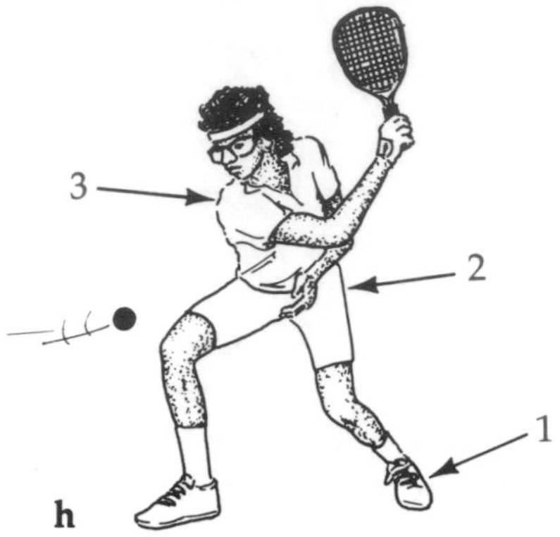

c

Backhand

h

i

_____ 1. Push off rear foot _____

_____ 2. Hips rotate forward _____

_____ 3. Shoulders face front corner _____

d

j

_____ 4. Racquet face comes perpendicular to intended line at contact _____

_____ 5. Wrist uncocks—thumb down _____

_____ 6. Arm is fully extended _____

_____ 7. Eyes are focused on ball _____

Follow-Through
Phase

Forehand   **Backhand**

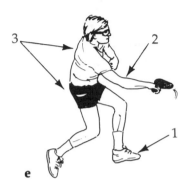

e   k

_____ 1. Weight shifts to front foot   _____
_____ 2. Racquet arm comes across
          body   _____
_____ 3. Shoulders and hips face front
          wall   _____

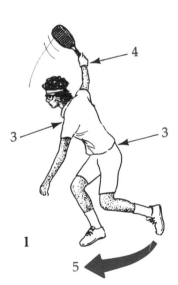

f   l

_____ 4. Wrist recocks after racquet
          strikes ball   _____
_____ 5. Bring back foot parallel to
          front foot   _____
_____ 6. Return to ready position   _____

Detecting Errors in the Basic Strokes

Everyone makes bad shots sometimes, and some of us make more than others. Your errors are usually determined by how much you play and practice. You should know that you can get better if you practice. But enlightened practice is much more productive, because sometimes you know you are not hitting good shots but may not know why. The following are some of the more common faults and possible corrections. You may want your instructor or a partner to observe you and help find the solution.

ERROR

CORRECTION

ERROR	CORRECTION
1. There is not enough time to hit. Can't get to the ball in time to gain balance and make a good shot.	1. Anticipate direction and depth of ball as it travels to the front wall. Don't wait until it bounces off the front wall. Move quickly to get into position.
2. The ball goes downward and hits the floor before it gets to the front wall.	2. This usually occurs more on backhand shots. Check your grip to be sure you changed from the forehand grip. Also be sure to transfer your weight forward with all your shots.
3. The ball goes too far left or right of the intended target.	3. Make sure you are contacting the ball near your front hip. This keeps the racquet face square.
4. Can't seem to hit the ball as hard as others.	4. Remember to shift your weight from rear to front. Continue to follow through. Don't swing at the ball—swing through it. Cock your wrist on the backswing and release it after contact. Practice the "Big Swoosh" Drill.
5. Generally lack control on shots.	5. Check for proper grip. Get into position earlier. Stroke the ball under control, don't hit it too hard. Be more conscious of your position relative to the ball. Keep your eyes focused on the ball. Choke up on the handle to help gain control. Improvement will come with practice.

Forehand and Backhand Drills

You will improve the control and quality of your shots in direct proportion to the amount you practice. There is no other way to improve your hand–eye coordination, positioning, weight transfer, and timing. Following are some basic drills to help you. Use some creativity and make up some of your own. Soon you will be playing short games as drills. That will make your practice more fun.

1. "Big Swoosh"

Practice your forehand and backhand strokes without a ball. Try to develop a smooth stroke with proper wrist action. If you get good wrist action and racquet head speed, you should hear your racquet "swoosh" at the moment you would be hitting the ball.

Success Goals = 50 total strokes

   a. 25 strokes with forehand swing

   b. 25 strokes with backhand swing

Your Scores =

   a. (#) _____ "swoosh" forehand swings

   b. (#) _____ "swoosh" backhand swings

2. Wall Rally

Stand behind the short line. Drop the ball to the floor. As it rebounds, hit it to the front wall. When it rebounds from the front wall, move into position and return the ball to the front wall again. Play it on any bounce. Do this as many consecutive times as you can without losing control. Use either your forehand or backhand stroke as necessary. Try to use good footwork when positioning yourself for the shot. Do not hit the ball hard. Just swing smoothly and keep the ball in play. Stay behind the short line.

   You can increase the difficulty of the drill by limiting yourself to only forehand returns. Further increase the difficulty by restricting yourself to backhand returns.

Success Goals =

   a. 20 consecutive returns without losing control

   b. 15 consecutive returns using forehand only

   c. 10 consecutive returns using backhand only

Your Scores =

a. (#) _____ consecutive returns—either stroke

b. (#) _____ consecutive returns—forehand only

c. (#) _____ consecutive returns—backhand only

3. Side-Wall Toss

Stand 4 to 5 feet from the side wall on your forehand side at midcourt. Toss the ball to the side wall 2 or 3 feet high. As the ball bounces, get into position and return it to the front wall with a forehand stroke. Next move to the backhand wall and practice.

Success Goals = 50 total returns to front wall

a. 25 forehands

b. 25 backhands

Your Scores =

a. (#) _____ forehands to front wall

b. (#) _____ backhands to front wall

4. Partner Forehand-Backhand

Both players stand near midcourt, one on each side of the midline (see Figure). The forehand player hits the ball off the front wall to the partner's backhand. The backhand player returns the ball to the partner's forehand side. The players try to keep the ball from hitting the side walls. Continue the rally for 20 hits (10 each). If you lose ball control, recover the ball and resume the drill until a total of 10 hits each has been reached. Then exchange sides for 20 more hits.

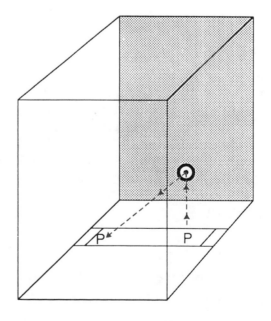

Success Goal = 20 consecutive hits, alternating forehands and backhands, with a partner

Your Score = (#) _____ consecutive forehands and backhands

5. Five-Point Partner Rally

Both players stand near center court. Player A drops the ball and hits it to the front wall. Player B tries to return it to the front wall before it strikes the floor twice. The rally continues until one player fails to return the ball. The other player then has scored one point. Player B then puts the ball into play. Play continues until one player has scored five points. Repeat for a total of three games.

Success Goal = Win 2 out of 3 games

Your Score = (#) _____ games won

Basic Strokes
Keys to Success Checklist

Now that you have learned and practiced the basic strokes, ask a friend or your instructor to watch you as you perform some of these drills. She or he can evaluate your technique according to the checklist items in Figure 3.2. A little time spent building a firm foundation here will enable you to get better faster. The next step will teach you the basics of serving, so you can start playing games and learn the game as you play, the natural and best way to learn.

Step 4 Beginner's Power Serve

Now that you know the basic strokes of the game, you are ready to start playing. Each point during a game starts with a serve. Some rules about racquetball serves are similar to those for tennis and badminton, but there are differences also. In this step you will learn the basic rules of serving and receiving and also how to execute and return the beginner's power serve. There are four basic serves you should learn to be a good player. The low power serve is the most basic. Lob, garbage (half-lob), and Z-serves are necessary to make you a complete player. More about those serves later. The beginner's power serve will help you start learning the game.

WHY IS THE SERVE IMPORTANT?

The serve is to racquetball what pitching is to baseball. Some estimate it to be as much as 80 to 90 percent of the game. In addition to scoring a point, a serve can set the tempo of the whole rally. It can immediately put the receiver on the defensive and force weak returns that the server can put away. Remember that only the server can score points. Unless you commit an out, you will have a second try at each point. This means you can take a few more chances for a "perfect" serve on the first attempt. The second attempt should be a "safe" one because you must put the ball in play to have a chance to score.

WHY IS RECEIVING THE SERVE IMPORTANT?

Because the server has the advantage, the ability to return serves is very important, just as it is in tennis. However, in tennis the serve alternates every other game. In racquetball, you must take the serve away from your opponent by your play. Unless you can do this, you will not have a chance to score points!

BASIC SERVING AND RECEIVING RULES

The server should announce the score before each service attempt. This prevents misunderstandings about the score. The server's score is always stated first. During service, both feet must be in the service area. The server's foot can be on, but not over, either line. If the ball should rebound and strike the server on the fly, the server is out. Remember that an out requires the server and receiver to exchange immediately. No second attempt at service is allowed. An out also occurs if the server misses the ball or the ball hits any other surface before it hits the front wall. If the serve lands on or in front of the short line when rebounding from the front wall, it is called a *short* and is a service fault. If the serve contacts the back wall before the floor, it is called a *long* and is also a service fault. A serve that contacts the ceiling after the front wall is a third type of service fault. Finally, a serve that contacts the front wall and then two side walls before contacting the floor is also a fault. Two consecutive service faults make an out, but faults do not accumulate. That is, once the ball is put into play by a legal serve, any prior fault ceases to exist.

The receiver may contact the serve on the fly or after one bounce. The receiver must be behind the receiving line until the serve is made and may not contact the serve in front of the short serve line. The receiver should be positioned near the imaginary midline and about 6 feet in front of the back wall. The return does not have to strike the front wall first, but must do so before striking the floor. In fact, some of the returns you will learn later must contact the ceiling or side wall first to be effective.

HOW TO EXECUTE THE BEGINNER'S POWER SERVE

To get started learning the game, beginners should start with a beginner's power serve. It will be easy for you to execute, because it is very similar to the forehand basic stroke. Stand in the center of the service zone with your shoulders facing the side wall and your nonracquet shoulder to the front wall. Your feet should be pointing toward the side wall or slightly toward the front corner. Hold your racquet with your forehand grip, far enough in front of you that when you shift your weight from your rear foot to your front foot, the ball is still in front of (nearer the front wall than) your front hip. How far in front of your hip the ball should be depends upon the angle at which you wish to direct the ball toward the front wall. Remember the angles you learned in Step 2. You want the ball to travel to the receiver's backhand side, so if you are right-handed and the receiver is also right-handed, the ball should return to your left side (see Figure 4.1). Your target should be slightly to the left of the center of the front wall if you are standing on the midline.

Your target should vary depending on where you are standing and the desired path of the serve. Later you will vary these factors to present different types of serves to the receiver. The target should be 4 to 6 feet high. This can also vary depending upon how hard you can, or wish, to hit the serve. You will want to vary these factors later, also. The constant factor is that you will want to hit the serve to the receiver's backhand most of the time. More about that in the next step. The ball must be contacted 4 to 12 inches forward of your front hip to direct the ball to your left. If the ball were contacted directly even with your front hip, the ball would come straight back toward you. If your opponent were left-handed, you would turn your body and contact the ball behind your front hip to direct the ball to the opponent's backhand. Finally, remember to keep your eye on the ball and follow through with your swing. Move to the center court position as quickly as possible after the serve (see Figure 4.2).

Set up in the ready position and anticipate your opponent's return. Do not look back. As you face the front wall, try to pick up the ball

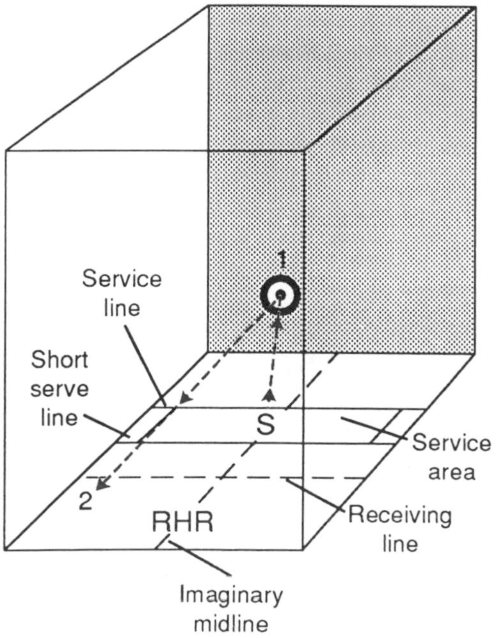

Figure 4.1 Beginner's power serve to a right-handed receiver.

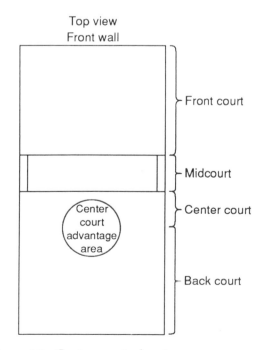

Figure 4.2 Center court advantage area.

with your peripheral vision. Looking back at your opponent's return has two disadvantages. First, you may be struck by the ball, and you most certainly do not want to get hit in the face. Second, you will not be able to react to the return in time to play it. Figure 4.3 shows the Keys to Success for the Beginner's Power Serve.

Figure 4.3 Keys to Success: Beginner's Power Serve

Preparation Phase

1. Forehand grip ____
2. Shoulders and feet facing side wall ____
3. Ball in fingers of nonracquet hand ____
4. Visualize target on the front wall ____

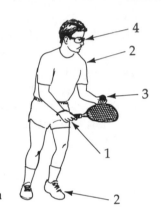

Execution Phase

1. Drop ball forward (4 to 12 inches) and to side (2 to 3 feet) ____
2. Step toward target with front foot ____
3. Start backswing with the first step ____

4. Push off rear foot ____
5. Keep eyes focused on ball ____
6. Contact ball in front of front hip ____

Follow-Through Phase

1. Continue swing through ball ____
2. Swing pulls shoulders and hips forward ____
3. Racquet arm comes across body ____
4. Rear foot moves to square body ____
5. Recover and move to center court ____
6. Head and eyes on the front wall ____
7. Assume ready position ____

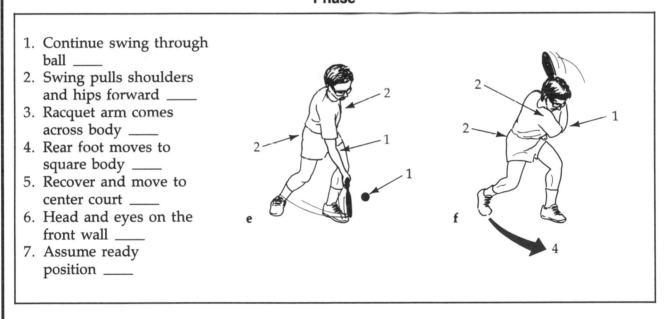

HOW TO RETURN THE BEGINNER'S POWER SERVE

Stand in a ready position on the midline, about 6 feet in front of the back wall (see Figure 4.4). Start with your backhand grip since the serve will probably come to that side. Do not stand near your backhand corner; a smart server will direct the serve to the open part of the court and you may not be able to reach the ball. Watch the ball closely during the serve. Don't be distracted by your opponent's body movements. Concentrate on returning the ball to the front wall (don't worry too much about where it goes). If you have time, direct the ball to the server's backhand side. Later, you will learn specific goals for returning the serve.

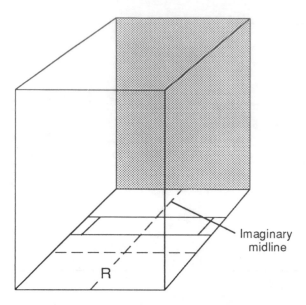

Figure 4.4 Receiving position.

Detecting Errors
in the Beginner's Power Serve

This serve is simple and only a foundation for a more advanced serve to come later. You will be able to correct most errors easily. Concentrate on hitting the ball to the receiver's backhand and putting the ball in play.

ERROR    **CORRECTION**

ERROR	CORRECTION
1. Serve lacks power.	1. Don't expect much. That comes later when you move your weight into the ball. Cock your wrist on the backswing and uncock your wrist on the follow-through. Strike the ball with the center of the racquet. Watch the ball closely while swinging.
2. Serve hits ceiling first.	2. Control face of the racquet. Racquet face should be perpendicular to the floor. Keep your racquet arm straight and drop the ball far enough away. Contact the ball waist high or lower.

ERROR   **CORRECTION**

3. Serve is too far right or left.

3. Ball is too far forward or too far back from front hip.

4. Ball is missed or serve hits floor before front wall.

4. Probably rushing your movements—get settled before attempt. Keep your eyes on the ball while swinging. Start your swing slowly and smoothly.

5. Ball hits side wall too soon and rebounds to center of court.

5. Move your target on the front wall more toward the center. Also move your starting position toward the center of the court if necessary. The ball may be too far in front of your front hip when contacted.

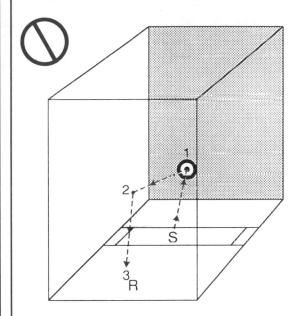

Beginner's Power Serve Drills

1. Ball Drop

Drop the ball forward and to the forehand side of your front hip and let the ball bounce a second time. The ball should land 8 to 12 inches forward of your front hip and 8 to 12 inches to the side.

Success Goal = 8 good drops out of 10 attempts

Your Score = (#) _____ good drops

2. *Serve to Receiver's Backhand*

Take your normal position and try to serve to the receiver's backhand corner. Remember that the ball must hit the front wall first and land behind the short line. It may hit one side wall and still be legal. Don't swing hard. Just direct the ball into the backhand corner. Then serve to the backhand corner of a left-handed receiver. Adjust your body angle and the position of the ball drop (farther back for right-handed server, farther forward for left-handed server).

Success Goals = 16 out of 20 total serve attempts to backhand

    a. 8 out of 10 serves to right-handed receiver's backhand

    b. 8 out of 10 serves to left-handed receiver's backhand

Your Scores =

    a. (#) ___ serves to backhand of right-handed receiver

    b. (#) ___ serves to backhand of left-handed receiver

3. *Quality Serves to Backhand*

The better quality serves to the backhand of a receiver are those that do not strike the side wall at all and bounce twice before contacting the back wall. The quality is still acceptable if the serve strikes the side wall deep in the court and/or the back wall no higher than 2 feet. If the serve strikes the side wall, it should be within 10 feet of the back wall. That would be 5 feet or more behind the receiving line.

When you develop better control and can hit quality serves with some regularity, you can challenge yourself further. Place a medium-size box (about 2 feet by 2 feet) in the back corner and try to hit the serve so it will hit the box on or before the second bounce. Be sure to place it in the other corner also, because you may play a left-handed player. A good-quality serve to the forehand can surprise a receiver who plays out of position expecting the serve to the backhand. Don't try to surprise them too often, however.

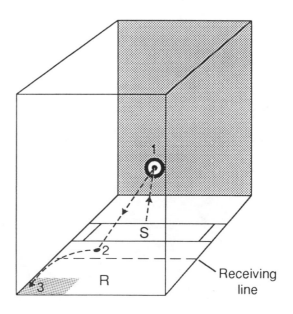

Success Goals =

    a. 5 quality serves out of 10 attempts to both corners

    b. 5 quality serves out of 10 attempts to box in both corners

Your Scores =

   a. (#) _____ quality serves to left-hand corner

      (#) _____ quality serves to right-hand corner

   b. (#) _____ quality serves to hit box in left-hand corner

      (#) _____ quality serves to hit box in right-hand corner

4. Serve and Return

Play a game with a partner, using only the serve and a return. The server gets one point for a serve to the backhand side. The server has two chances at each point, unless she or he commits an out. The receiver gets a point for every legal return to the front wall. Do not continue the rally. It is over when the receiver makes the return attempt. The first player to score seven points wins the game. Switch server and receiver roles after each game. The receiver should be positioned about a half step to the backhand side of the imaginary midline and three steps forward of the back wall. The server should remember to call out the score before each service attempt.

Success Goal = Win at least 3 out of 6 games

Your Score =   (#) _____ wins, (#) _____ losses

Beginner's Power Serve Keys to Success Checklist

Now that you have reached the Success Goals for the beginner's power serve, repeat Drill 3, and ask an experienced racquetball observer to evaluate your serving technique according to the checklist in Figure 4.3. Don't worry about serving hard or perfect serves. Just try to put the ball in play. If you get it correct right now, you will improve on your serves later.

Figure 4.5 (on page 46) lists some of the important facts about faults and outs that can oc-cur on service attempts. Beginners sometimes get confused about the difference between faults and outs. Don't worry too much about that. If you are not sure whether a service error is a fault or an out, talk it over. If you still can't decide, ask an experienced player or your instructor. If no one is available, just replay the serve and look it up later. As you play more, it gets much easier to distinguish between faults and outs.

	Out	*Fault*
When does it happen?	Can occur on either first or second attempt.	Can occur on either first or second attempt.
What is the result?	No further attempt is allowed.	After first fault, one more is allowed. Two faults make an out.
How does it occur?	Any time service attempt does not strike front wall first.	Many types—all after service attempt has hit front wall first.
Special names or occurrences.	Whiff or miss, rebound hits server on fly, crotch serve.	Short, long, three-wall, ceiling.

Figure 4.5 Faults and outs on service attempts.

Step 5   Strategy Rule #1— Hit It to Their Backhand

This is the first of six basic rules of strategy that will help you to become a better player. In addition to learning this rule, you will learn enough to start playing games. A short rules quiz will help you get ready. Then the exercise at the end will encourage you to get started on putting this rule into practice. Drills and practice are necessary to improve your skills but playing short games can show you the importance of having these skills. In addition to being more fun, playing the game can help teach you to think and apply shots while playing. You will notice that many of the advanced drills are designed to get you to think and react in a game-like situation. This is the best way to learn to apply the basic rules of strategy.

WHY IS STRATEGY RULE #1 IMPORTANT?

You might think that this rule is too elementary to mention. Yet all players appear to go through various stages when they learn racquetball. The first stage is to merely return the ball to the front wall without regard to where it will go from there. Many beginners serve 50 to 70 percent of their serves to their opponent's forehand. The alert player will soon realize that returns from the opponent's backhand are weaker and often result in no legal return at all. Neophytes should hit 90 to 95 percent of their shots to the opponent's backhand. If your opponent starts playing out of position, you can often score a winner by directing your shot to his or her forehand. So Rule #1 is "Hit It to Their Backhand." This includes your serves as you practiced them in Step 4. When you can do this regularly, you are through stage one and will improve rapidly as a racquetball player. This rule will be valid as long as you play the game.

HOW TO EXECUTE STRATEGY RULE #1

The best way to learn this rule is by playing in a game situation and hitting the ball to your opponent's backhand. You know how to serve and hit the basic forehand and backhand shots. They are the basis of just about all the shots you will develop as a player. They are certainly enough to start playing and learning more about the game. This is also when you start having fun. Fun and enjoyment should be part of learning any new activity. Remember, you are just starting a new activity, so don't worry if you haven't learned all the angles and shots. Just play and have a good time while you are learning the game. To play a game, you will need to keep score, and the following quiz will help prepare you for that.

SCORING READINESS

Answer the following questions to see whether you are ready to start keeping score. Refer to the sections describing the game and the beginner's power serve to refresh your memory. The answers follow the quiz.

Rules Quiz

1. When the server announces the score as 1–5, who is leading?

2. The server is struck by the ball while in the service area after the serve has bounced once. What is the ruling?

3. The receiver at center court returns the serve on the fly. What is the ruling?

4. The serve contacts the front wall, then the ceiling, then lands in front of the short serve line. Fault or out?

5. The serve contacts the front wall, then the ceiling, then lands behind the short serve line. Legal serve, fault, or out?

6. The server tosses the ball into the air (as in a tennis serve) and serves an otherwise legal serve. Is this a legal serve?

7. The serve contacts the ceiling, then the front wall, then lands forward of the short serve line. Legal serve, fault, or out?

8. The serve contacts the front wall, then the back wall, then the floor behind the short serve line. Legal serve, fault, or out?

9. The server swings at a serve but misses. Retry, fault, or out?

10. The serve contacts the floor, then the front wall, then rebounds to land on the floor behind the short serve line. Legal serve, fault, or out?

Answers to Rules Quiz

1. Receiver.
2. Fault—short serve.
3. Legal return—ball is in play.
4. Fault—as soon as it hits the ceiling.
5. Fault—as soon as it hits the ceiling.
6. No, the ball must bounce in the service area first. The server is out.
7. Out—the serve did not hit front wall first.
8. Fault—long serve.
9. Out.
10. Out—the serve did not hit the front wall first.

Hit to Their Backhand Drill

Now you are ready to play a game and concentrate on hitting the ball to your opponent's backhand. Don't worry about whether you win or lose the game. But if you are losing, ask yourself whether you are using Strategy Rule #1—''Hit It to Their Backhand.''

Practice Game

You will need a third person for this game. Two will play, and the third will act as an observer from outside the court. Paper and pencil will help you keep track of the information you need for this activity.

Play a game to seven points. The observer counts the number of shots (including serves) that you hit to your opponent's backhand. She or he also counts the number of shots to the forehand. All three take turns being the observer. This means you will play two games but will have your hits counted in only one. If you are in a class, or have four people in your group, both players can be evaluated during the same game. Concentrate on directing your shots to your opponent's backhand. You can repeat this activity for as many games as you wish, using the following procedures:

a. Record:

   Number to backhand ＿＿＿   Number to forehand ＿＿＿   Total number ＿＿＿

b. Calculate percentage:

$$\text{Percent} = \frac{\text{Number of shots to backhand}}{\text{Total number of shots}}$$

Success Goal = 75 percent of all shots to opponent's backhand

Your Score = (%) ＿＿＿ of all shots to backhand of opponent

Step 6   Lob Serve

The lob serve is one of the four basic serves and is the most underutilized of all the serves. It is hit high and softly against the front wall, takes a high bounce after hitting just behind the short serve line, and then dies in the rear corner. Because it is not hit hard, many beginners view it as a weak serve. This is far from the truth. Develop a good lob serve, and you will have a valuable tool to help you control the tempo of the game. There are several variations of the lob serve. The cross-court lob and the garbage lob (half-lob) are the two most common. These are executed by varying the angle and height of the serve. You will learn both of these modifications in this step.

WHY IS THE LOB SERVE IMPORTANT?

It is true that few aces are scored on lob serves, but advanced players recognize that it is a valuable weapon. It can be used to make aggressive players overanxious. They don't like to wait for the lob serve. This soft serve can also cause them to commit unforced errors as they try to hit shots that have a low chance for success. It can also change the pace of the game from rapid to slow. This will disrupt many players' patience and concentration. Finally, it can be used to elicit a poor return that the server can then put away for a point. Many receivers try to return the lob serve with an offensive shot, and set the alert server up with an opportunity to score while the receiver is still deep in the backcourt. In addition to all this, it is a very safe serve for a second service attempt. The lob serve is more difficult to execute than it appears, but with a little practice you can become skilled enough to take advantage of this off-speed serve. By developing the cross-court lob and the garbage lob, you will be able to keep the receiver off-balance. She or he will not know which serve you plan until the last minute. By changing the angle and bounce of the serve, you will cause the receiver to adjust to the differences. With a variety of serves available, you will be able to keep the receiver off-balance.

HOW TO EXECUTE THE LOB SERVE

Face the front wall with your toes pointing straight ahead, 3 to 5 feet from the side wall. Bounce the ball high enough with your non-racquet hand to enable you to move underneath the ball and contact it high above the level of your head. The ball should be contacted with an overhead stroke at a point about 3 or 4 feet higher than your racquet shoulder and about 1 foot in front of your body. Your weight should be on your rear foot as you take your backswing and transfer smoothly to your front foot at contact. The forehand grip should be used, and the raquet face should be nearly square to the front wall at contact. Deviations will affect the direction and height of the serve. Figure 6.1, a-e, shows the Keys to Success for the overhead stroke lob serve.

The lob serve can also be executed with a sidearm stroke (see Figure 6.1, f-k). Beginners often do this because it is easier to bounce the ball for a serve. Advanced players use it for a change-up because it changes the angles of the bounces for the receiver. You do not have to master the overhand stroke before attempting either the sidearm or the underhand stroke.

Figure 6.1 Keys to Success:
Lob Serves

**Preparation
Phase**

Overhead Stroke Lob Serve

Sidearm Stroke Lob Serve

____ 1. Bounce ball to right and
      forward   ____

____ 2. Start backswing—racquet be-
      hind elbow   ____

____ 3. Step forward—eyes on ball   ____

Execution
Phase

Overhead Stroke Lob Serve

Sidearm Stroke Lob Serve

h

d

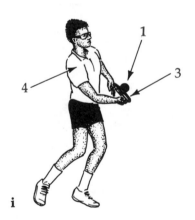

i

____ 1. Strike ball gently   ____
____ 2. Wrist leading racquet   ____
____ 3. Racquet face open   ____
____ 4. Shoulders rotate forward ____

Follow-Through Phase

Overhead Stroke Lob Serve

Sidearm Stroke Lob Serve

j

k

e

_____ 1. Weight shifts from rear to front
_____
_____ 2. Wrist does not break
_____
_____ 3. Recover balance—move to center court
_____

HOW TO POSITION EFFECTIVELY

To serve to a right-handed receiver you should position yourself 4 or 5 feet from the left wall. The target for your serve should be within 3 feet of the side wall and within 4 feet of the ceiling. The ball should be struck with great control and not much force. Up to this point, the footwork and mechanics of the lob serve resemble the serve in tennis. Of course you must bounce the ball off the floor instead of tossing it into the air. Then, unlike the tennis serve, you strike the ball softly and hit it upward with an open racquet face. The ball should bounce 2 to 5 feet behind the short serve line and then again before striking the back wall. The best lob serves will be within 1 foot of the side wall and never strike the side wall. This is why they are sometimes called *down-the-line lob serves.* Acceptable lob serves can strike the side wall deep in the court—within 5 feet of the rear wall. They may also strike the rear wall before the second bounce but should hit no more than 3 feet high (see Figure 6.2a).

You can serve the same serve to a left-handed receiver by moving to a position near the right side wall (see Figure 6.2b). This serve is actually easier for a right-handed server to execute. You must contact the ball a little more to the right of your body, and the racquet face should be square to the front wall or even facing a little to the right. Because the racquet is on the same side as the wall, it is much easier to keep the ball from contacting the side wall (down the line).

WHEN TO USE LOB SERVES

Lob serves are effective only to the receiver's backhand. They should never be attempted to the receiver's forehand. Even when served toward the receiver's backhand, there are three disadvantages to lob serves. When served from near the side wall, a slight error can result in the ball contacting the side wall first. This results in an out and no chance of scoring points. A second disadvantage is that the server tends to remain in the serving area and does not move to a good offensive position. It takes special concentration to move into position after a lob serve. A third problem can arise if your serve hits the side wall after rebounding from the front wall. If it hits the side wall in front of, or near, the center of the court, it will then rebound out toward the midline of the court. This sets up the receiver to attempt an offensive shot rather than having to return with a defensive shot.

GARBAGE LOB SERVE

This serve is also called the *half-lob serve* and is a modification of the lob serve. The ball is contacted lower and struck with more force. It also is not as weak a serve as some might think. Rather, it is a more advanced serve that can be used to force the receiver to return the ball from shoulder or chest height. This

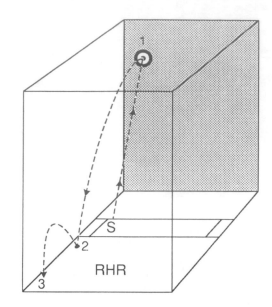

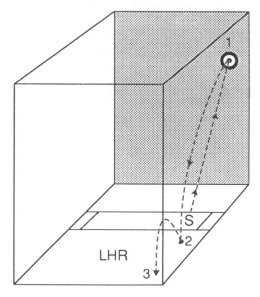

Figure 6.2 Serve position from the left side (a) to a right-handed receiver, or from the right side (b) to a left-handed receiver.

serve limits the receiver's selection of return shots. The garbage serve can be executed from the side wall position or from a center court position (see Figure 6.3, a and b). Be sure to hit the ball with enough force so the receiver must play the ball at shoulder height. Too little force might let the receiver hit a low kill or low passing shot from near the knee. Too much force might let the receiver play the ball off the back wall with the same type of returns.

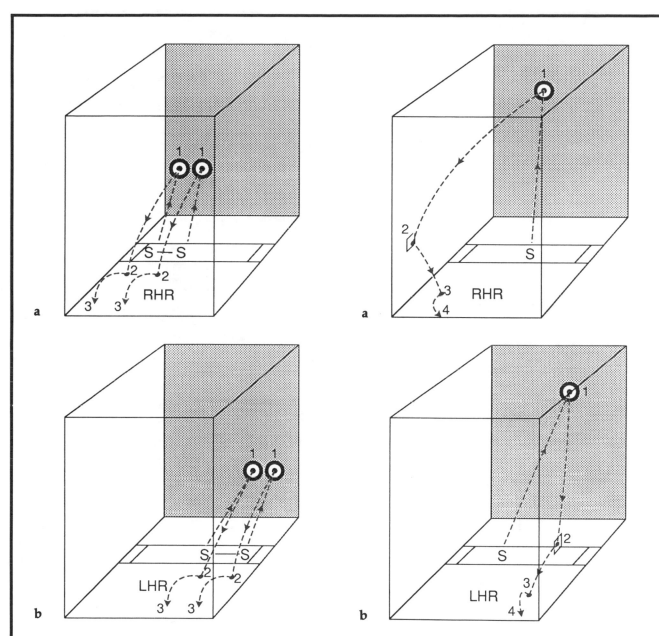

Figure 6.3 The garbage serve from either the side wall position or center court position for both a right-handed receiver (a) and a left-handed receiver (b).

Figure 6.4 Lob serve from center court to right-handed receiver (a) and to left-handed receiver (b).

CROSS-COURT LOB SERVE

Another modification of the lob serve is to change the position from which one serves. Many prefer to stand near the center of the service area. The serve is then angled so that it contacts the side wall near the corner before it hits the floor (see Figure 6.4, a and b). A great deal of touch is required to insure that the ball dies in the corner. The advantage is that the server is near center court and can set up quickly for the next shot. This serve can be executed with an overhead or underhand stroke.

Detecting Errors
in the Lob Serve

Most errors with the lob serve are due to lack of concentration. Because it is a soft serve, many beginners fail to focus their attention on their goals and targets. You must be sure to give this serve your full attention, and it will give you many easy setups in return. Try the following suggestions, and with a little practice and concentration you should master this valuable serve.

ERROR

CORRECTION

1. Ball hits side wall too soon.

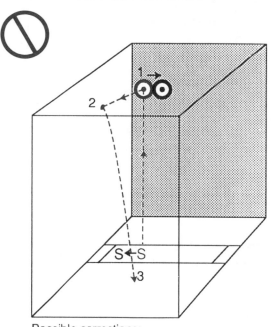

Possible corrections:
1. Move target away from side wall
2. Move starting position toward wall

1. Move starting position closer to side wall. Change front wall target so ball hits farther from side wall. Change angle of racquet face at contact. Bounce ball more to side of body.

2. Serve hits ceiling.

2. Racquet face should close more. Ball should be contacted farther in front of body. Let the ball drop a little more before contacting it.

ERROR   **CORRECTION**

3. Ball hits too far from side wall.

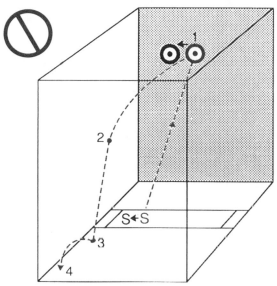

Possible corrections:
1. Move target closer to side wall
2. Move starting position toward side wall

3. Move starting position closer to side wall. Move target closer to side wall. Change angle of racquet face at contact. Ball may be too far to side of body. Move closer to ball, or drop ball closer.

4. Ball hits back wall before second bounce.

5. Ball hits close to short line but doesn't bounce deep enough.

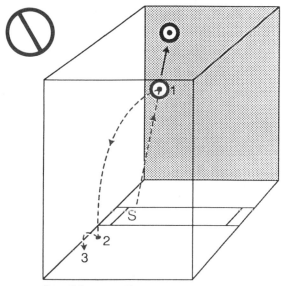

Possible corrections:
1. Hit ball with more force
2. Move target higher on front wall

4. Hit ball with less force and/or lower on the front wall.

5. Hit ball with more force and/or higher on the front wall.

Lob Serve Drills

1. Ball Bounce

Bounce the ball with downward force hard enough that ball goes 2 or 3 feet higher than your head. Let the ball bounce a second time. The ball should land 8 to 12 inches in front of your right foot.

Success Goal = 7 good bounces out of 10 attempts

Your Score = (#) _____ good bounces

2. Lob Serve (Down-the-Line) to Corner

Stand within 4 or 5 feet of the left side wall. Use either an overhand or a sidearm stroke. Your target on the front wall should be about 3 feet from the side wall and 4 feet from the ceiling. As it rebounds, the ball should not hit the side wall at all, or it should not hit it until it is within 5 feet of the back wall. The ball should bounce twice before hitting the back wall or strike the back wall no higher than 3 feet before the second bounce. Next, move to the midline serving position and try the cross-court lob serve. Your front wall target should be about 4 feet from the ceiling and 2 or 3 feet left of center. This varies with your serving position, so experiment with your target and starting positions to find the location that works best for you. Next, try a lob serve to your right-hand corner. Remember, you may play a left-hander. You must adjust your serving position to a spot near the right side wall (4 to 5 feet). Use either an overhead or a sidearm stroke.

Success Goals = 6 good serves out of 10 attempts to each corner from each serving position

Your Scores =

a. (#) _____ good serves to left-hand corner (down the line)

b. (#) _____ good serves to left-hand corner (cross court)

c. (#) _____ good serves to right-hand corner (down the line)

d. (#) _____ good serves to right-hand corner (cross court)

3. Garbage Lob Serve to Corner

Stand near the side wall or in the center of the service area. This drill is very similar to the lob serve drill. The difference is in the greater amount of force with which you strike the ball—and, of course, in the fact that your target then must be much lower on the front wall. It is, however, a very different serve and should be practiced separately. Bounce the ball about shoulder height for the overhead stroke, then hit the ball with medium force aiming to the left-hand corner. Bounce the ball about waist height for the sidearm stroke. The ball should strike the front wall about 8 feet high. As it rebounds from the front wall, the ball bounces once and hits the back wall about 2 feet high. If you are working with a partner, the receiver should let the serve go to the back wall. Both should then observe how high the ball hits on the back wall. Adjust the force of your serve accordingly. You want to force the receiver to play the ball at shoulder height. The ball should hit near the corner—3 or 4 feet to either side would be acceptable. Now try a garbage lob to the right-hand corner. If you are right-handed, you must change the angle of your body slightly to direct the ball into the right-hand corner.

Success Goals =   7 good serves out of 10 attempts to each corner from each serving
   position

Your Scores =
   a. (#) _____ good serves to right corner (down the line)
   b. (#) _____ good serves to right corner (cross court)
   c. (#) _____ good serves to left corner (down the line)
   d. (#) _____ good serves to left corner (cross court)

4. Partner Return Lob Serve

The receiver assumes a position on the midline about 6 feet forward of the back wall and tries to return a lob serve to her or his backhand corner with any type of shot. Do not continue play. The receiver then gives the server feedback on the quality of the serve. The server must be sure never to look back, but to quickly assume a position at center court. Serve five serves, then exchange positions. Repeat once more. Repeat again with the server serving a garbage lob serve.

Success Goals =   7 out of 10 lob serves returned (two types)

Your Scores =
   a. (#) _____ of 10 lob serves returned
   b. (#) _____ of 10 garbage lob serves returned

5. Lob Serve Game Situation

Play a game to seven points. Both players serve only lob serves. Give each other feedback after the game about quality of serves. Down-the-line serves should be close to the side wall. Cross-court serves should die in the corner. In no case should the receiver be able to play the serve with a forehand stroke. Repeat as often as time allows.

Success Goal = 2 games played

Your Score = (#) _____ games played

Lob Serve
Keys to Success Checklist

The lob serves you have learned in this step will be valuable to you for the rest of your playing days. They are not used as often as the power serve you will learn next. You may then ask why they were covered first. The answer is twofold. First, the lob serve is easier on your arm and elbow. Many beginners do not have the power or control to serve hard. The lob serves give you an effective serve to enjoy the game while developing your muscular conditioning and control. Secondly, most aggressive persons tend to forget about using the lob serve. To develop it first should im-press you with its effectiveness and get you started in the habit of using some lob serves. Don't hesitate to use the lob serves often. Years ago, I lost a championship tournament match to a player who used only lob serves—a lesson I will never forget! There are so many variations of delivery, angles, and power that you could serve an entire game and never give the receiver the same serve twice.

Ask your instructor or a friend to evaluate your serves using the checklist in Figure 6.1 as a guide. Work on the fundamentals to build a solid foundation for the future.

Step 7 Power Serve

This serve is also called the *power angle serve* or the *drive serve*. It is different from the beginner's serve in that it is lower and harder. To get the power, you must move within the service area to get increased weight shift. High-ability players use this as their basic serve and can usually score a considerable number of aces with it. The forehand stroke you developed in Step 3 is the stroke used for the power serve.

WHY IS THE POWER SERVE IMPORTANT?

This serve is used most of the time by experienced racquetball players. It is the serve used when a player wants to score an ace. Even when it does not produce an ace, a hard serve allows the receiver little time to make a return. Thus, you may get a weak return that you can put away. Serving from different angles and with different speeds gives an unlimited number of possibilities, which can cause many adjustment problems for the receiver.

HOW TO EXECUTE THE POWER SERVE

This serve is done with a sidearm version of your forehand stroke (see Figure 7.1, a-f). Good players move toward the front wall while serving and hit the ball low and hard. Start near the short serve line, facing the side wall. Your nonracquet foot should be about 6 inches nearer the front wall and slightly nearer the side wall you are facing. Your weight should be evenly balanced. The ball is held loosely in your fingers with your arm hanging at your side. You should have your forehand grip with the racquet hanging loosely near the floor. Glance at the V of your hand to see if it is on the top back bevel. Also glance back to check the receiver's position. Start your movement toward the front wall with a crossover step with your rear foot (right foot if right-handed). Your rear foot should stay be-hind your front foot in a crossover fashion, but move 12 to 18 inches toward the front wall. Now your weight shifts to your rear foot as you place it down. At the same time, reach out and drop the ball low—about 6 to 10 inches above the floor and in front of the body. It should be about 2 feet in front of the body and 2 feet toward the side wall, depending upon the length of your arm and racquet. Now step toward the front wall with your front foot.

Your racquet should have started back as you were reaching out to drop the ball. It should be behind you with your wrist cocked and your thumb pointing up toward the ceiling. Your knees should be bent and your body low. Your eyes have been on the ball since you started to drop it. Push off your rear foot as your arm starts the forward swing. Because you want to keep your body low, your swing is sidearm with your arm parallel to the floor. Your eyes are still focused on the ball when you contact it near the top of the bounce, about 8 to 10 inches off the floor. The ball should hit 1 to 3 feet high on the front wall, depending on how hard you hit it. The harder you hit it, the lower it should hit the front wall. Your arm comes toward the front wall and then across your body as you contact the ball, and your wrist releases.

Your rear foot should come around and forward as your hips and shoulders continue their rotation. You should be facing the front wall as you finish. Recover your balance and get ready to play your opponent's return. You may move anywhere in the service area as you serve. Your feet may be on, but not over, either line. A violation is a service fault, called a *foot fault*.

The serve should be to the receiver's backhand and low enough to bounce twice before contacting the back wall. The most effective serves do not contact the side wall, although they can be effective if they don't contact the side wall until deep in the court. Deep would be within 5 to 7 feet of the rear wall. The server can make the serves more effective by changing the angle. This is done by starting the serve a different distance from the side wall. More complexity can be added by varying the power.

The server must remain in the service zone until the ball passes the short line. This is not usually hard to do. The opposite is usually the case. You must train yourself to quickly move to the center court area about 3 to 5 feet behind the short line. The normal tendency is to stand and watch the serve, but you must train yourself to move. When you reach the center court area, face the front wall and assume the ready position. If you anticipate the receiver's return you can quickly gain the advantage.

Figure 7.1 Keys to Success: Power Serve

Preparation Phase

1. Weight shifts to front foot ____
2. Rear foot moves toward front wall ____
3. Drop ball low in front of body ____
4. Weight transfers to rear foot ____
5. Front foot moves toward front wall ____
6. Racquet arm starts back slowly ____
7. Wrist cocks at top ____
8. Body is low—knees bent ____
9. Eyes on ball ____

**Execution
Phase**

1. Body stays low—knees
   bent ____
2. Weight transfers to front
   foot ____
3. Racquet arm comes
   forward—wrist
   uncocks ____

4. Contact ball low—8 to 10
   inches ____
5. Sidearm swing ____
6. Eyes remain on ball ____
7. Ball contacts front wall
   low—1 to 3 feet ____

**Follow-Through
Phase**

1. Arm continues across
   body ____
2. Wrist releases ____
3. Rear foot comes forward
   and up ____
4. Hips and shoulders face
   front wall ____
5. Recover balance—ready
   to move ____

RETURN OF THE POWER SERVE

One reason the power serve is used so much is that it is difficult to return. The difficulty increases if the serve is low and hard and placed along the backhand wall. Sometimes when the serve goes into the corner, it is hard to tell how the serve will come out of the corner. You can minimize this problem if you will follow these guidelines. First, stay on the midline. If you set up too near your backhand corner, the server can sneak a serve into your forehand corner and you will never reach it. Additionally, you will have trouble adjusting to the rebound from the corner if you are too close. If you must overplay your backhand, do so by no more than half a step. Second, stay 6 to 8 feet in front of the back wall. Turn and touch the back wall with your racquet and arm extended. Then take 1 or 2 steps toward the front wall. Now, if the serve goes into the backhand corner, turn to face the corner while watching the ball closely. If the ball rebounds close to the side wall, you should be able to catch up to it. If it hits the side wall first and rebounds toward the midline, you can make a pivot and return the serve with a forehand stroke after it rebounds from the back wall.

Another option the receiver has from this position is to cut the serve off before it gets to the corner. That will depend upon many things, including the speed and angle of the serve and the ability of the receiver. You can increase your chances by anticipating a serve to your backhand and starting with a backhand grip. At the beginning level, you should concentrate on just returning the serve to the front wall. Later, you can consider returning the serve with a passing shot or a ceiling shot. They will be discussed in Steps 9 and 10.

The third guideline is to watch the ball the whole time and resist the temptation to watch the server. Watching the server's body or arm movement cuts down on the reaction time you have to return the serve and makes it almost impossible to return a quality serve.

Detecting Errors in the Power Serve

Because this serve is so basic and so important, you should practice it as much as you can. Most players try to hit the ball too hard. Work on your control first. Power will come as you practice. Many beginners rush their movements trying to generate more power. Many also have trouble staying low while moving. It takes time and a lot of practice to develop a low, hard power serve.

ERROR

CORRECTION

ERROR	CORRECTION
1. Serve lacks power.	1. Don't expect too much at first. Move your body in the direction you want the ball to go.
2. Serve hits too far right of the front wall target.	2. Drop the ball closer to the front wall and/or farther left.
3. Serve hits too far left of the front wall target.	3. Drop the ball farther back from the front wall and/or farther right.
4. Serves are too high.	4. Keep your knees bent. Drop the ball lower.
5. General inconsistency.	5. Keep your eyes on the ball. Don't rush your swing.

ERROR 🚫	CORRECTION
6. Serve hits the side wall too soon.	6. Move the front wall target away from the corner. Drop the ball closer to your front hip. Move your body forward while swinging.
7. Serve hits the back wall before the second bounce.	7. Move the target lower on the front wall. Drop the ball from a lower height and contact it lower. Keep your body lower.
8. Serve is too far from the side wall.	8. Move the target on the front wall closer to the corner. Move your starting position closer to the side wall.

Power Serve Drills

1. Footwork

Review the Keys to Success in Figure 7.1, a-f, for the power serve. Now, without a ball, go through the footwork. Have a partner work with you and check each other. Start with feet close together. Stay low and move forward, completing your footwork within the service area. Swing your racquet to help you get the timing of the swing with the steps.

Success Goal = 20 times done properly

Your Score = (#) _____ times done properly

2. Ball Drop

This drill is a progression of the footwork drill. Repeat the footwork, but drop a ball from your nonracquet hand as you move your rear foot. As you complete your footwork, reach out and forward and catch the ball with your racquet hand. Square your body to the front wall with the ball in your hand.

Success Goal = 20 ball drops and catches

Your Score = (#) _____ times ball caught in hand

3. Power Serve to Back Left-Hand Corner

Remember that serves to the backhand will be most effective and that most receivers are right-handed. From a position about 4 to 6 feet from the left side wall, hit a power serve that does not hit the side wall and bounces twice before it reaches the back wall. It should not contact the front wall higher than 3 feet. The harder you hit the ball, the lower it must contact the front wall. To further increase your accuracy, set a medium-size box (about 2 feet by 2 feet) in the corner. Try to have the ball hit the box.

Success Goals = 5 out of 10 power serves as previously described

Your Scores =

   a. (#) _____ good serves out of 10 tries to the corner

   b. (#) _____ good serves out of 10 tries to the box

4. Power Serve to Back Right-Hand Corner

From a position midway between the side walls, hit a power serve to the right rear corner. The serve is executed in basically the same way as the serve to the left-hand corner. The major difference is the direction of the steps and body movement. It should be slightly toward the right-hand corner instead of straight forward. The criteria are the same. The ball should bounce twice before reaching the rear wall, should not hit the side wall, and should hit the front wall lower than a height of 3 feet. Next, set a medium-size box (about 2 feet by 2 feet) in the corner. Try to have the ball hit the box.

Success Goals = 5 out of 10 power serves as previously described

Your Scores =

   a. (#) _____ out of 10 tries to the corner

   b. (#) _____ out of 10 tries to the box

5. Return of Power Serve

The server serves to the backhand corner, trying to make good serves. The receiver should be positioned three steps forward of the back wall and no more than a half step to the backhand side of the imaginary midline. The receiver scores one point for every serve returned. The server scores one point for every ace. The server does not play the receiver's return. The first player to reach five points wins the game. Then exchange positions for another game. The server is allowed to serve to the forehand if the receiver is playing out of position.

Success Goal = Win at least half of the games played

Your Score = (#) _____ wins; (#) _____ losses

Power Serve
Keys to Success Checklist

As you get ready for someone to evaluate your power serve, work on your tempo so you develop a smooth, coordinated movement. You should think of the serve as one continuous, smooth act, and not as separate parts that you put together. If you can do this, you can concentrate more on the ball and make a more powerful swing without rushing or swinging too hard. Ask your evaluator to use the Keys to Success items in Figure 7.1 to help you determine what you need to work on.

Step 8   Strategy Rule #2— I Own Center Court

The center court position is equally distant from the side walls and 3 to 5 feet behind the short line. It is a general area indicated by the circle in Figure 8.1 and can vary slightly according to the opponents or other situations.

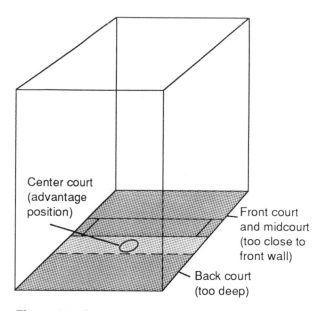

Figure 8.1 Center court position.

WHY IS THE CENTER COURT POSITION IMPORTANT?

The player who occupies the center court position usually is in control of that particular rally or exchange of shots. The intelligent player learns quickly that from this position she or he can hit kill shots (low shots that stay up front) when the opponent is deep. Likewise, you can hit passing shots (shots that stay close to the side wall) when the opponent tries to come up to center court after a shot from deep in the court. You will learn more about these shots and how to hit them in Steps 9 and 12.

HOW TO EXECUTE STRATEGY RULE #2

Utilizing this rule to the fullest extent requires two separate skills. The first is quickly moving to the center court position after every shot (even a serve). The natural tendency is to stand and watch your shot after you hit it. You must develop the habit of moving quickly toward center court after every shot, even if it means retreating back to where you just hit the previous shot. You cannot adequately cover all areas of the court in any other way.

The second skill is having shots that will move your opponent out of the center court if he or she also knows the "secret" Rule #2. Passing shots and ceiling shots (especially to the backhand) are two effective shots for accomplishing this goal. These shots are described in Steps 9 and 10. Practice them and you will have two valuable tools to help you gain the center court advantage.

Center Court Drills

1. Wall Touch

Start at center court. Run and touch one side wall with your racquet. Use a shuffle step. Return to the ready position at center court, then shuffle to the other side wall. Return to center court. Using a crossover step, turn and run to the back wall. Watch the front wall all the time over your shoulder. Touch the back wall and return to center court. Run to touch the front wall. Cross over and run back to center court while watching the front wall over your shoulder. Set up at center court again.
  Repeat 2 more times.

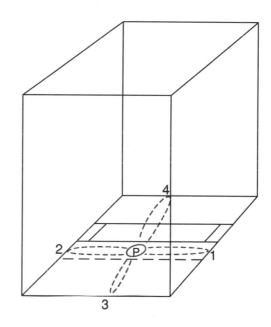

Success Goal = 3 repetitions of touching walls and returning to ready position at center court

Your Score = (#) _____ repetitions

2. "Simon Says"

With a partner behind you, set up at center court. The partner calls which wall to go to (right, left, front, back). Run to a position near that wall and take an imaginary swing at the ball (remember to change grips). Return to set up at center court as quickly as possible. Watch the front wall while returning. Repeat five times, then exchange roles with partner.

Success Goal = 6 reaction drills

Your Score = (#) _____ reaction drills

3. X Marks the Spot

Mark an X on the center court position with tape. Alternate turns at service. Play a game using regular rules, except for keeping score. Points are scored by touching the X with your feet during the rally. You get one point each time you touch the X at center court. First player to 15 wins the game. Play five games.

Success Goal = Win 3 or more games out of 5

Your Score = (#) ____ of games won out of 5

4. I Own Center Court

Play a game to seven points. Have an observer count the number of shots you hit, including serves. The observer also counts the number of times you return to center court after each shot. Use the following procedures:

a. Record:

Number times returned to center court after each shot ____

Total number shots hit ____

b. Calculate percentage:

$$\text{Percent} = \frac{\text{Times returned to center court}}{\text{Total shots hit}}$$

Success Goal = 90 percent of the time return to or toward center court

Your Score = (%) ____ times returned to center court

Step 9 Passing Shots

A passing shot is a shot that goes past your opponent so she or he cannot reach the ball. This shot has two purposes. The first is to force your opponent to vacate a position at center court. The second is to score a point when your opponent leaves an opening because of poor court position. Another time you can use the passing shot to score a point is when your opponent is a little late in coming back to center court from the back wall. If she or he is rushing too much, your opponent will not have time to recover and retrieve the passing shot unless it is a very poor one.

WHY ARE THE PASSING SHOTS IMPORTANT?

This shot is one of the basic and most often used shots in racquetball. It can be used both as an offensive weapon to score points and as a defensive technique to gain center court position. You can keep your opponent off-balance with passing shots, and it is one of the most effective ways to make an opponent vacate center court. By learning to vary the angle and the speed of the shot, you can force your opponents to adjust their style of play. Long rallies in which players must retrieve many shots can be boring and frustrating to a power player who likes to hit kill shots, and long rallies also work to your advantage when you are in better physical condition than your opponent.

HOW TO EXECUTE THE PASSING SHOTS

The passing shot is usually hit when your opponent is in front of you or beside you so that you can see his or her position on the court. This position and the position of the ball dictate which type of passing shot to hit. The two types are explained in the following sections. The mechanics used in executing the passing shots are the forehand and backhand strokes that you learned in Step 3.

Down-the-Line Pass

If your opponent is nearer one side wall and you are hitting the ball on the open side, try a down-the-line passing shot. A down-the-line pass hits the front wall near the side wall and rebounds toward the back wall, staying near the side wall. The angle changes depending upon where you hit the ball from, but generally the down-the-line pass always stays on one side of the court, never crossing the imaginary midline. To hit this shot, hit the front wall at an angle that bisects the open part (away from your opponent) of the front wall (see Figure 9.1, a and b). You can use either a forehand or a backhand stroke. The ideal shot is hit with enough velocity to get past the opponent but not enough to hit the back wall before bouncing twice. The harder you hit the shot, the lower on the front wall it should hit. In no case should it hit the back wall before hitting the floor twice. It also should not hit the side wall. Most down-the-line passes should be hit with only one half to three quarters of your power so your opponent does not have a chance to play it off the back wall. Beginners usually hit the ball too high and/or too hard and set their opponent up for an easy return off the back wall. Most down-the-line passes should hit the front wall from 1 to 3 feet high, depending on how hard they are hit.

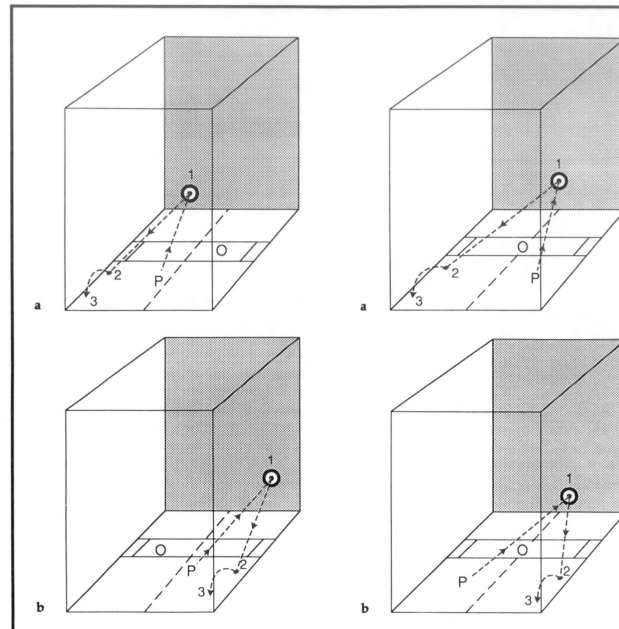

Figure 9.1 Down-the-line passing shots from the left side (a) and from the right side (b).

Figure 9.2 Cross-court passing shots from the right side (a) and from the left side (b).

Cross-Court Pass

If your opponent is near the midline, you may wish to try a cross-court passing shot (see Figure 9.2, a and b). This shot is hit so that the ball rebounds to the opposite side of your opponent. The angle will vary with your position, but the ball should be hit so that it will go past your opponent before contacting the side wall. It also should die before contacting the back wall.

WHEN TO USE THE PASSING SHOTS

The keys to which passing shot to use are the position of your opponent and the position where you must play the ball. Keep in mind that the passing shot is rarely used when you are in front of your opponent. Kill shots (Step 12), Z-shots and around-the-wall shots (Step 17), and ceiling shots (Step 10) are usually used in these instances. If you get drawn up to the front court and your opponent comes up fast to center court, a down-the-line passing shot is a good option and an exception to the rule. Following are some illustrations of which passing shots to use in certain situations.

When Your Opponent is Near the Midline

When your opponent is near the midline and in front of you, always use the cross-court pass (see Figure 9.2, a and b). If you and your opponent are both in center court and your opponent is near the midline, you could use either the cross-court or the down-the-line pass (see Figure 9.3, a and b). In this case, the deciding factor would be to direct it to the opponent's backhand. When your opponent is in the backcourt, any type of passing shot is a low-percentage shot. Do not try it.

When Your Opponent Is Near a Wall

When your opponent is near either wall and at center court or closer to the front wall, you have an opening. Even a mediocre down-the-line pass will be effective in these situations (see Figure 9.4, a-d). This is the obvious choice. Don't hit any other shot in this situation. Remember two important points: Don't let the ball hit the side wall, and hit the ball hard enough to get past your opponent but not so hard that it contacts the back wall before bouncing twice. This is a situation you wait for. Capitalize on it.

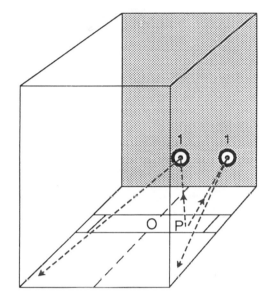

a

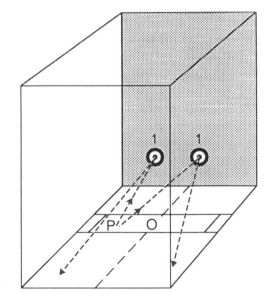

b

Figure 9.3 Passing shots from center court from the right (a) and from the left (b).

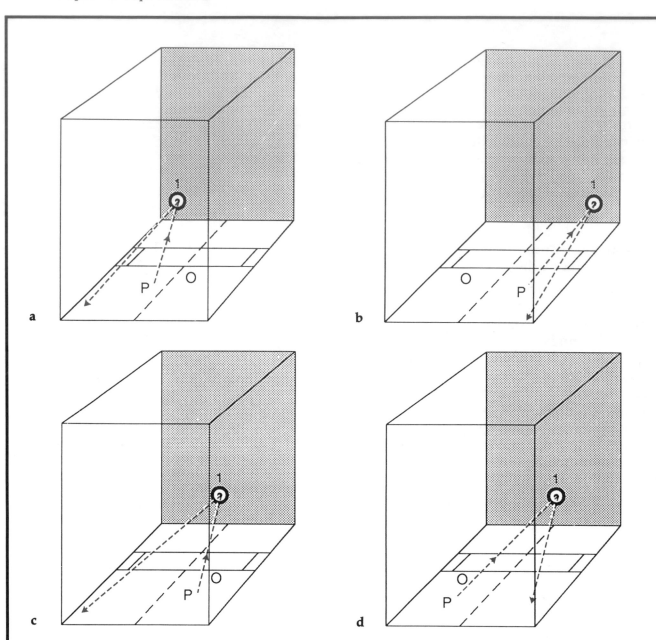

Figure 9.4 Passing shots when your opponent is near a side wall with player on left and opponent on right (a), player on right and opponent on left (b), both on right (c), and both on left (d).

Detecting Errors in Passing Shots

Most of the errors committed on passing shots are caused by swinging too hard or without thought about the purpose of a passing shot. Both faults are more mental than physical. Study the errors and corrections to learn the concepts. Practice the passing shot drills to train yourself to think while you are executing.

ERROR 	CORRECTION
1. The ball hits the side wall and rebounds toward the midline.	1. Change the angle of your racquet face. Move your target more toward the center of the front wall—away from the corner. Don't swing so hard. Concentrate on direction and placement.
2. The ball hits the back wall after one bounce and rebounds into midcourt or center court.	2. Don't swing hard. The ball must die in the backcourt. Hit the ball lower on the front wall.
3. Shots are inconsistent right and left.	3. Make sure you have a proper grip. Make sure you have the proper position on the ball. Don't swing so hard. Concentrate on direction and placement.
4. You do not attempt passing shots. You use other shots or just try to hit the ball back to the front wall.	4. This is a natural part of the learning process. You must have confidence in your forehand and backhand strokes before you can advance to the next level. Practice more on your forehand and backhand drills. Increased skill will lead to increased time to think about what type of return to attempt. Be patient with yourself.
5. Wrong type of passing shot is attempted.	5. Don't worry too much. We all do this. Make a mental note of it. Also practice Drill 6—''Decision Time.''

Passing Shot Drills

1. Down-the-Line Passes

Stand near a side wall and in the service area. Place a box in the service area on the midline to make this drill more realistic. A person standing there with outstretched arms would be even better. Hit a down-the-line passing shot that stays near the wall without hitting it. Use your forehand stroke. Keep the ball in play by hitting consecutive passes. Next, use your backhand stroke near the other side wall. This is much more difficult. Be sure to have good body position. Take a smooth, controlled swing. Don't swing too hard. Placement is much more important than power here.

Success Goals =

a. 8 consecutive forehand down-the-line passes

b. 6 consecutive backhand down-the-line passes

Your Scores =

a. (#) ____ consecutive forehand down-the-line passes

b. (#) ____ consecutive backhand down-the-line passes

Next, move back into the center court area. Repeat the forehand and backhand down-the-line passes. This increases the difficulty, but you will need to be able to hit good passes from here.

Success Goals =

a. 6 consecutive forehand down-the-line passes

b. 4 consecutive backhand down-the-line passes

Your Scores =

a. (#) ____ consecutive forehand down-the-line passes

b. (#) ____ consecutive backhand down-the-line passes

Finally, move to the backcourt. Move the box (or the friend) back to the center court position. You need more power here, but don't sacrifice your control. This is a hard drill, but that's exactly why you need to practice this shot.

Success Goals =

a. 3 consecutive forehand down-the-line passes

b. 2 consecutive backhand down-the-line passes

Your Scores =

a. (#) ____ consecutive forehand down-the-line passes

b. (#) ____ consecutive backhand down-the-line passes

2. Partner Down-the-Line Passes

With a partner, alternate hitting down-the-line passing shots. Stay on the forehand side. If the ball touches the side wall, that ends the drill. Next, repeat the drill on the backhand side.

Success Goals =

a. 12 consecutive passing shots on the forehand side

b. 8 consecutive passing shots on the backhand side

Your Scores =

a. (#) _____ consecutive passing shots to forehand side

b. (#) _____ consecutive passing shots to backhand side

3. Cross-Court Pass

Standing in the service area, start with a forehand pass to your backhand side. Move quickly to return the ball with a backhand pass to your forehand side. Control the velocity so it is possible to reach the ball. Put a medium-size box on the midline so you can visualize the angle necessary to pass someone. If you are working with a partner, the partner can stand in that area with both arms outstretched to give you a better idea of the angles. Next, try this from the center court area. The box (or partner) is moved back to the center court area. Finally, to increase the difficulty, attempt these passes from the backcourt area. Leave the box (or partner) in the center court position.

Success Goals =

a. 10 consecutive passing shots from service area (5 each way)

b. 8 consecutive passing shots from center court (4 each way)

c. 6 consecutive passing shots from backcourt (3 each way)

Your Scores =

a. (#) _____ consecutive passing shots (service area)

b. (#) _____ consecutive passing shots (center court)

c. (#) _____ consecutive passing shots (backcourt)

4. Partner Cross-Court Pass

With a partner, stand in center court near opposite side walls. Hit cross-court passes to each other. One partner hits forehand and the other hits backhand. Continue until one misses, then change places and repeat.

Success Goal = 20 consecutive cross-court passes (after each player has done drill both ways)

Your Score = (#) _____ consecutive cross-court passes

5. Advanced Passing

Here is a drill you can do by yourself. It also makes a good warm-up. Start in the center court area. Start with a down-the-line pass on your forehand side. Return with another one. Continue for five shots, then hit a soft cross-court pass. Quickly move to cut it off and return it with a down-the-line pass on the backhand side. Continue for five shots, then repeat the entire drill.

Success Goal = 2 complete cycles of the drill (24 shots)

Your Score = (#) _____ completed passing shots

6. Decision Time

Here is a drill to help you decide which passing shot to use in a game-like situation. You need a partner for this drill. Player A starts the rally with an easy shot to the front wall. Player B returns it with another easy shot near the center of the court. Player A then hits another easy return and yells "Now!" Player A then takes a position near the midline or either side wall, and Player B tries to pass Player A with the appropriate pass (review Figures 9.1 through 9.4). Player A tries to return the passing shot. Player B gets one point for a successful pass. Player A gets one point for returning the attempted pass. The first player to get five points wins the game. Then exchange roles. Play six games.

Success Goal = Win 4 out of 6 games

Your Score = (#) _____ games won

7. The Passing Game

Start like a regular game. The difference is that you alternate serves regardless of who wins the rally. Winning the rally does not necessarily score a point. If the rally ends with an error, missed shot, or anything but a quality passing shot, you simply change serving order. The only way you can score a point is with a quality passing shot—that is, a pass that hits the floor twice before it gets to the back wall. Play the passing game to five points. Then start a new game. Play five games.

Success Goal = Win 3 out of 5 games

Your Score = (#) _____ games won

Step 10 Ceiling Shots

The ceiling shot is probably the most under-used shot in racquetball. The ball hits the ceiling 2 to 5 feet from the front wall, hits the front wall, bounces on the floor in the front court, and then takes a high arc toward the back wall. If it hits the back wall, the effective ceiling shot does so near the floor, coming down at a sharp angle that would make a return difficult for any player. There is also a variation of the ceiling shot that hits the front wall before the ceiling. And as you might expect, you will learn to hit ceiling shots with your forehand and backhand strokes.

WHY ARE CEILING SHOTS IMPORTANT?

The ceiling shot is effective for driving your opponent out of the center court area and allowing you to gain the momentum of the rally. It is considered a defensive shot and is not intended to end the rally. However, placing a good ceiling shot to an opponent's backhand corner can often win the rally, especially if the opponent is not highly skilled. Still, the main purpose is to drive the opponent out of position and hope for a weak return you can put away to end the rally.

The best return of a good ceiling shot is another ceiling shot. In fact, often that is the only possible return, so you will frequently see veteran players get into long rallies of ceiling shots until one makes a mistake and the other tries to capitalize on it. Your opponent will likely know Strategy Rules #1 and #2, so you should develop a good ceiling shot if you want to become a good player. You should also develop the ability to return a ceiling shot with another ceiling shot using your backhand stroke.

HOW TO EXECUTE THE FOREHAND CEILING SHOT

The first step is to move quickly into position, like an outfielder about to catch a fly ball. You will want to hit the shot with your forehand, if possible. Get under the ball so it is 2 to 3 feet above your racquet shoulder. It should be slightly in front of you so you can step into the shot and get enough weight transfer and power into it. Take your racquet back behind your shoulder as you approach the ball. This will give you more time to make a stroke without being rushed. Keep your eyes focused on the ball during the entire time you are moving. You can pick up your opponent and the walls with your peripheral vision. It should be easier to anticipate your opponent's movement now that you know the center court strategy rule.

As you are getting into final position, your backswing should have rotated your hips slightly toward the side wall. Your back foot may also be pointed toward the side wall with most of your weight on it. Your front foot has very little weight on it, so you can step toward the front wall with your shot. As you do so, your arm swing starts with your elbow leading. Your wrist stays cocked until you hit the ball. The ball should be above and in front of your shoulder so you have to reach up and out as you swing. Your racquet face will be slightly open so as to direct the ball upward to hit the ceiling about 2 to 5 feet from the front wall (see Figure 10.1). This depends on your position in the court. If you are very deep in the court, you may have to aim your ceiling shot to hit more than 5 feet back from the front wall. As your position is nearer the front wall, the ball must be hit nearer the front wall.

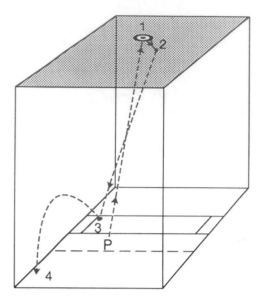

Figure 10.1 Initial target for ceiling shots.

It is critical to keep your eyes on the ball all through the swing. As your weight shifts to your front foot, your rear foot comes forward to square your body, stop your momentum, and gain your balance. Your wrist has released, and your arm swing continues forward and down, sometimes across your body if you are returning the ball at an angle. Your eyes should not follow the ball past your position.

Concentrate on moving toward the center court position and anticipating the return from your opponent. Figure 10.2, a-d, shows the Forehand Ceiling Shot Keys to Success.

HOW TO EXECUTE THE BACKHAND CEILING SHOT

The backhand ceiling shot is hit in much the same way as the forehand ceiling shot. Proper position with regard to the ball, watching the ball intently, and good weight transfer are all the same. The backhand ceiling shot is much more difficult to hit (see Figure 10.2, e-h). The rotation of the hips and shoulders is exaggerated. Your toes point toward the side wall, and your shoulders and hips face the side wall. Your arm comes across your body, and your racquet is behind your shoulder, pointing down toward the floor. The ball is contacted farther back in relation to the body, again depending upon the angle at which you wish to return the ball. Usually you will try to return it along the wall on your backhand side. This means that the ball will be contacted almost even with the midline of your body (as you are facing the side wall; see Figure 10.2g).

Figure 10.2 Keys to Success:
Forehand and Backhand Ceiling Shots

**Preparation
Phase**

Forehand Ceiling Shot   **Backhand Ceiling Shot**

_____ 1. Move quickly into position   _____
_____ 2. Take racquet back behind
          body   _____
_____ 3. Eyes focused on ball   _____

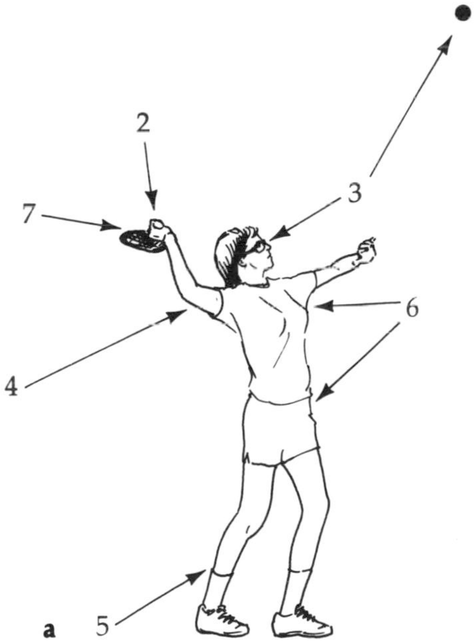

4. Racquet arm bent—
   racquet behind
   shoulder _____

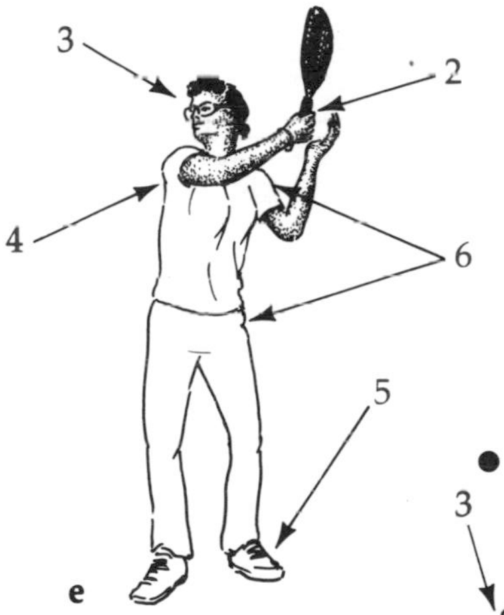

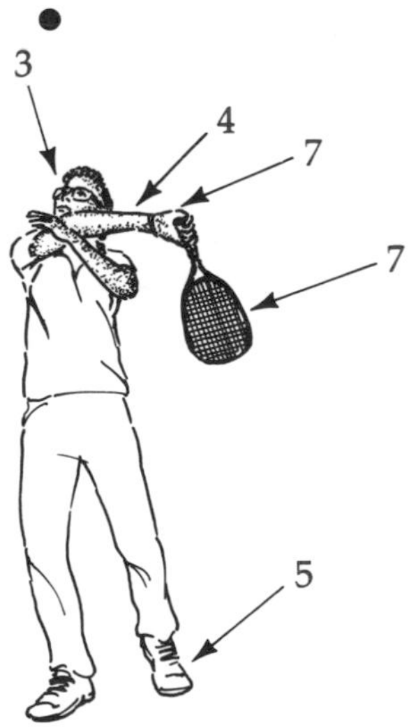

4. Racquet arm across
   body—elbow high _____

_____ 5. Weight mostly on rear foot   _____
_____ 6. Shoulders and hips toward
          side wall   _____
_____ 7. Wrist cocked—racquet head
          points down   _____

Execution Phase

Forehand Ceiling Shot   **Backhand Ceiling Shot**

_____ 1. Push off rear foot _____

_____ 2. Arm swings forward—elbow leads _____

_____ 3. Wrist stays cocked until contact _____

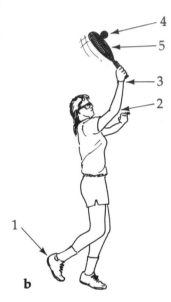

b

4. Contact ball above racquet shoulder _____

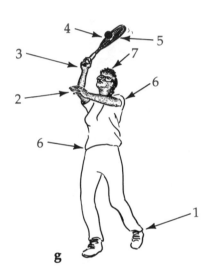

g

4. Contact ball above center of body _____

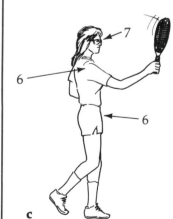

c

_____ 5. Racquet face slightly open vertically _____

_____ 6. Shoulders and hips rotate forward _____

_____ 7. Eyes remain fixed on ball _____

_____ 8. Target 2 to 5 feet from front wall _____

**Follow-Through
Phase**

Forehand Ceiling Shot   **Backhand Ceiling Shot**

1. Weight shifts mostly to front
____   foot   ____

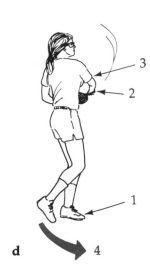

d   h

2. Wrist releases forward   2. Wrist releases toward
   and down ____   back of hand ____
3. Arm swings forward and   3. Arm swings across
   down ____   body ____

____ 4. Rear foot comes forward   ____
____ 5. Regain balance to both feet ____
____ 6. Get ready to move quickly ____

Detecting Errors
in the Ceiling Shots

The most common error in executing ceiling shots is failure to have the correct position relative to the ball. The stroke mechanics are usually easier to learn. The backhand ceiling shot takes a lot of practice to master. Here are some common problems and suggestions to correct them.

ERROR **CORRECTION**

ERROR	CORRECTION
1. The ball hits the ceiling but doesn't get to the front wall.	1. Move your target closer to the front wall. Move your body position back farther so the ball is more in front (forward) of your body on contact. Close the face of the racquet.
2. The ball hits the side wall (too far right or left).	2. Move the target away from the side wall toward the center line. Make sure the ball is in front of or slightly outside your shoulder and not in the center of your body or too far outside when it is contacted.
3. The ball rebounds too far off the rear wall.	3. Hit the ball with less force—about 50 to 75 percent of full force. Also try to move your target a little closer to the front wall.
4. The ball hits the front wall—it doesn't get to the ceiling.	4. The ball is contacted too low or too far in front of your body. Your body should be only slightly behind the ball. Open the racquet face more.
5. The ball doesn't get deep enough to the backcourt.	5. Hit the ball with more force. Move the target closer to the front wall.

FRONT WALL CEILING SHOT

You will soon discover that there is another way to execute the ceiling shot. When the ball strikes the front wall first, and then the ceiling, this imparts a spin to the ball that causes it to bounce differently. The ball will bounce more straight up and down. If it does get to the back wall, it will tend to slide down the wall instead of bouncing out toward the center. This causes a real problem of adjustment for the returner, who must be aware of this difference and concentrate intently to avoid making a mistake in positioning for the shot. You should be able to hit this shot intentionally whenever you want. A good idea is to use it after an exchange of two or three regular ceiling shots to try to create an adjustment problem for your opponent. It is very difficult to hit this shot from deep in the court, so use it sparingly and wisely. Your percentage for an effective shot increases as your position moves toward center court. You may also use a sidearm or underhand stroke to make this shot.

Figure 10.3 shows the approximate target when the shot is executed from center court. The actual target can vary depending upon your position on the court. This will in turn affect the angles and heights of the bounces.

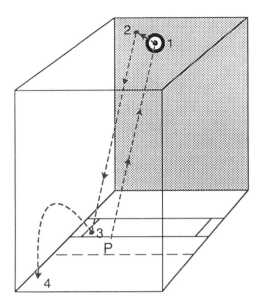

Figure 10.3 Initial target for front wall ceiling shot executed from center court.

Ceiling Shot Drills

1. Phantom Ball

Do this drill with your racquet, but without a ball. Imagine you are executing a ceiling shot. Say to yourself, "Look up, push off back foot, swing." This will help you to feel the weight transfer. It can be practiced anywhere.

Success Goals = 50 phantom swings for both forehand and backhand

Your Scores =

    a. (#) _____ forehand ceiling shot swings

    b. (#) _____ backhand ceiling shot swings

2. Bounce-and-Hit Ceiling Shots

From center court, either throw the ball up or bounce it hard on the floor. Get into position quickly and execute a ceiling shot. Direct it toward the backhand corner of a right-handed player. Remember to aim to hit the ceiling about 5 feet from the front wall. Then try to direct the shot to the other corner as practice for playing left-handed players.

Success Goals = 8 out of 10 attempts properly executed and directed to each corner

Your Scores =

  a. (#) _____ good shots of 10 attempts to left-hand corner

  b. (#) _____ good shots of 10 attempts to right-hand corner

3. Ceiling Shot in a Cardboard Box

Same drill as previously given but use a medium-size (about 2 feet by 2 feet) cardboard box against back wall as a target.

Success Goals = 5 out of 10 attempts into box in each corner

Your Scores =

  a. (#) _____ in box in left-hand corner

  b. (#) _____ in box in right-hand corner

4. Ceiling Shot Rally

Start in midcourt or backcourt. Hit a ceiling shot and then try to return it with another ceiling shot. Hit as many consecutive ceiling shots as possible. You can have four different goals when practicing this drill:

  a. Initially, just try to keep the ball in play with consecutive ceiling shots. Use your forehand or backhand stroke, whichever is necessary.

  b. Hit all forehand ceiling shots to your forehand side. Now you are trying to control the direction in addition to hitting the ball the proper depth. Concentrate hard on controlling the angle of the face of your racquet. Use about one half to three quarters of your power. Remember, you want the ball to die in the back corner. Of course, if you hit perfect shots, you won't be able to keep the ball in play.

  c. Now try to hit all backhand ceiling shots to your backhand corner. This is much more difficult, so don't get discouraged. Lower your goals. If you can hit three consecutive backhand ceiling shots to your backhand corner, you have good control. It is important to be able to hit this shot, because your opponent will certainly hit ceiling shots to your backhand and you will want to hit one in return most of the time. The person who can do this will have a great advantage in any game.

  d. Alternate forehand and backhand ceiling shots, directing them to opposite sides of the court. You will not use these angles as much in a game, but it will be helpful to be able to hit these cross-court ceiling shots. The forehand cross-court ceiling shot will be used more often to hit to your opponent's backhand. The backhand cross-court ceiling shot will go to the backhand of a left-handed player (that is, if you are right-handed).

Success Goals =

a. 8 consecutive ceiling shots

b. 6 consecutive forehand side ceiling shots

c. 3 consecutive backhand side ceiling shots

d. 6 consecutive ceiling shots alternating forehand and backhand

Your Scores =

a. (#) _____ consecutive ceiling shots

b. (#) _____ consecutive ceiling shots to forehand

c. (#) _____ consecutive ceiling shots to backhand

d. (#) _____ consecutive ceiling shots alternating forehand and backhand

5. *Partner Ceiling Shot Rally*

Both players stand in midcourt near the midline. One player starts with a ceiling shot. The other player returns it with a ceiling shot. Keep the ball near the midline of the court. Try to keep the ball in play using any of the ceiling shots you have practiced. This drill is excellent for improving your skill. It can also be used as a warm-up prior to playing a game. Next, try to direct your ceiling shots to the opposite corner each time. You probably wouldn't do this in a game, especially if you were going to hit it to your opponent's forehand corner. However, it is a good drill for practicing control. Finally, try to sustain a rally using ceiling shots only to your partner's backhand corner. This is more difficult, but worth the practice time.

Success Goals =

a. 12 consecutive ceiling shots

b. 8 consecutive ceiling shots to alternate corner

c. 6 consecutive ceiling shots to backhand corner

Your Scores =

a. (#) _____ consecutive ceiling shots

b. (#) _____ consecutive ceiling shots to alternate corner

c. (#) _____ consecutive ceiling shots to backhand corner

Ceiling Shots
Keys to Success Checklists

The ceiling shots are difficult to execute but very valuable, so the effort to learn to hit a good one will pay handsome dividends. Ask your instructor or a trained observer to evaluate your technique according to the checklist items in Figure 10.2. Your observer should pay particular attention to how quickly you get back into proper position under the ball so you have ample time to get a good weight shift. You are encouraged to run around your backhand to hit the ceiling shot with your forehand. Of course, if you do this, you must make sure you make an extra effort to hurry back to center court position. It is worth taking yourself a little out of position to be able to hit this shot with your forehand.

Step 11 Strategy Rule #3—Love the Back Wall

This rule is to remind you to sometimes let the ball go past you, rebound from the back wall, and then play it. There are many advantages to following this rule. If you follow it and master (love) the back wall, you will be on your way.

WHY IS THE BACK WALL IMPORTANT?

Racquetball is unique in that players can let the ball pass them and still have a chance to keep it in play. In fact, better players soon learn that there are many advantages to this strategy. It is not easy to do, however. Even if you overcome the instinct to play the ball as soon as possible, you may be in for some major frustration. Often you will misjudge the direction or the distance the ball will rebound from the back wall. Don't let yourself get discouraged. You will never progress past a low level of ability unless you develop this skill, so the sooner you start, the faster you will progress.

HOW TO PLAY THE BACK WALL

The decision to let the ball go to the back wall is the first step in the process. If you have had time to set up in the center court position, your opponent may try to hit a passing shot. If the ball comes to you at waist height or higher, you probably should let the ball go to the back wall. At other times, you will have no choice but to go to the back wall, because you will not be able to reach the ball before it gets past you.

There are two types of bounces you will get off the back wall. In the first, the ball comes almost straight back to the back wall from the front wall. It will rebound almost straight toward the front wall. Your adjustment here is to decide how far from the back wall it will rebound and then get into proper position.

Unless the ball has acquired spin from the racquet or a previous wall, its rebound angle will be equal to its approach angle (see Figure 11.1). This rebound will tend to come farther toward the center court area and will not be hard to estimate. Try to position yourself inside the angled path of the ball and estimate where you will play the ball (see Figure 11.2). Get to that position quickly. If you do, you will have time to adjust your position slightly if necessary.

The second and more difficult return is the shot that has hit a side wall and rebounds from the back wall at a greater angle (see Figure 11.3). It may also have picked up some spin from the racquet or a side wall. Notice how it rebounds

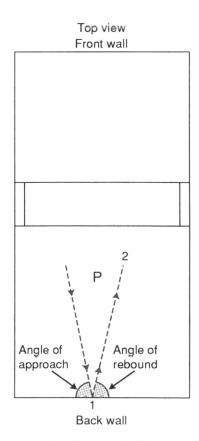

Figure 11.1 Angle of rebound off the back wall typically equals the angle of approach.

Front wall

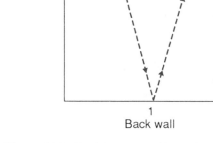

Back wall

Figure 11.2 Position yourself inside the angled path of the ball to return the ball off the back wall.

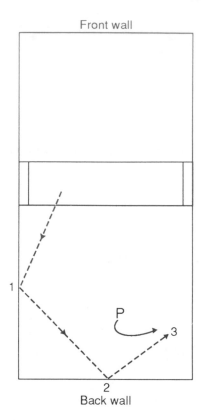

Front wall

Back wall

Figure 11.3 Angle of approach from a side wall to the back wall causes the ball to rebound at more of an angle off the back wall.

more toward the side wall and tends to stay in the backcourt. To play these shots, it is important that you stay inside the angled path of the ball. You must turn and follow the ball with your eyes. Do not chase the ball, however; you will never catch it. Instead, pivot like a basketball player and estimate the path of the ball. Take a shorter route inside the angle and go to meet the ball. Again, you may have to make a slight adjustment, so get there early if you can. This shot becomes even more complex when you realize the ball could be traveling toward your backhand side (see Figure 11.4).

Here is a summary of the principles that will help you progress faster.

1. Always keep your eye on the ball. This means never turn your back to the ball or let it go behind you. If you must turn to follow the ball, pivot like a basketball player and always keep the ball in sight.

2. Don't chase the ball—go to meet it. Try to estimate where it will be and go to that spot quickly. Then you may have to make a final adjustment to the ball. Sometimes this means moving toward the ball, but it can also mean moving away from the ball so you have room for a good arm extension and swing.

3. The third principle is related to the first two. As you are turning and moving, stay away from the walls and out of the corners. Most of your initial movement should be along the midline.

4. Wait for the ball to drop before hitting it. Beginners often rush their shots because they do not realize how much time they really have to complete the shot. How far you let the ball drop depends upon the type of shot you plan to hit. The important thing to remember is that this habit will give you additional time to settle yourself and plan a good shot.

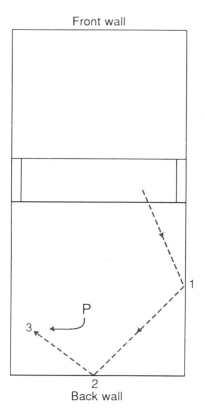

Front wall

P

3

1

2

Back wall

Figure 11.4 Side wall, back wall angled rebound to a right-handed player's backhand.

LOVE THE BACK WALL

This is the central concept of racquetball and the way it is played and enjoyed by millions. Give yourself time to learn the angles and bounces, and you will be building a strong foundation for your future as a good racquetball player. Sometimes when your opponent hits a passing shot, your only chance is to play it off the back wall. You should also look for the opportunity to play shots off the back wall. This will give you more time to determine where your opponent is located and to plan your shots.

You may wonder what type of shot to hit off the back wall. You can hit any type of shot you wish, but the best choice will be determined by your opponent's location and the position where you must play the ball. Steps 9 and 10 gave you guidelines about when to hit the passing shots and ceiling shots. Guidelines for other types of shots are given in the appropriate steps. Whichever shot you choose, the summary information in the following Keys to Success will help you learn the angles and procedures needed to love the back wall (see Figure 11.5).

Figure 11.5 Keys to Success: Back Wall Play

Preparation Phase

1. Make decision—let ball (waist-high or higher) go to wall ____
2. Follow ball with eyes ____
3. Turn with ball ____
4. Move to general area quickly ____
5. Go to meet ball—don't chase it ____
6. Know where opponent is ____
7. Plan what shot to hit ____
8. Start backswing early ____

Execution Phase

1. Keep eyes on ball ____
2. Make final adjustment to ball ____
3. Wait for ball to drop low enough ____
4. Make forehand or backhand stroke ____
5. Move with shot ____

Follow-Through Phase

1. Regain balance ____
2. Move quickly toward center court ____
3. Assume ready position ____
4. Anticipate return ____
5. Don't look back ____

Detecting Errors in Back Wall Play

Some pick up the concept of letting the ball go past them right away. Others are reluctant to let it go. Don't worry, you will make some wrong decisions, but that is how you learn.

The speed, height, and angle of the ball's path all affect the decision. Soon you will be able to decide whether the ball is going to be playable off the back wall.

ERROR ⊘

CORRECTION

1. Not enough time to hit.

1. Anticipate the path of the ball and go to meet it—don't follow it. You may have to run away from the back wall as the ball is going toward the back wall.

ERROR	CORRECTION
2. Can't get to the ball fast enough, especially on angled rebounds	2. Pivot like a basketball player. Watch the ball as you pivot. Remember, the ball leaves the back wall at an angle equal to its approach angle. Take the inside path.
3. Ball rebounds from back wall right at you (too close).	3. Don't worry, you are in the first stages of learning the back wall play. Quickly back away the length of your arm plus the racquet. Let the ball drop as you do, and you will have time to play it.

Back Wall Drills

1. Back Wall Toss

Stand 5 or 6 feet from the back wall. Toss a ball 3 or 4 feet high on the back wall. Let it bounce once, and then return it to the front wall with a forehand stroke. Then repeat the drill, tossing the ball so you must return it with a backhand stroke.

Success Goals =

    a. 25 forehand returns to front wall

    b. 25 backhand returns to front wall

Your Scores =

    a. (#) _____ forehand returns to front wall

    b. (#) _____ backhand returns to front wall

2. Back Wall Setup

From the middle of the court, stroke the ball to the front wall high enough and hard enough that it will bounce once and then carom off the back wall. Position yourself so that you can hit the ball to the front wall before it bounces a second time. Repeat for a total of 10 times. Next, stroke the ball with your forehand to set yourself up, but try to return it with a backhand shot.

Success Goals =

  a. 7 of 10 successful forehand returns each way

  b. 7 of 10 successful backhand returns each way

Your Scores =

  a. (#) _____ of 10 successful forehand returns

  b. (#) _____ of 10 successful backhand returns

3. Continuous Back Wall Setup

Try to keep the ball continuously in play off the back wall by striking your return in such a way as to keep the ball coming off the back wall. Use either forehand or backhand strokes as necessary. Then try it using only forehand strokes. Finally, try it using only backhand strokes.

Success Goals =

  a. 10 continuous returns

  b. 7 continuous forehand returns

  c. 5 continuous backhand returns

Your Scores =

  a. (#) _____ continuous returns either way

  b. (#) _____ continuous forehand returns

  c. (#) _____ continuous backhand returns

4. Chase the Rabbit

Hit a shot to the front wall, then run to play a return after any number of bounces. Try to hit the shots high and hard enough so they will get to the back wall. Don't worry if you can't get to the ball before the second bounce. This drill will help you learn the angles. It also is a good warm-up and a good conditioner. You must play the ball before it crosses the short line on its way to the front wall after rebounding from the back wall.

Success Goal = 5 minutes chasing the rabbit

Your Score = (#) _____ minutes chasing the rabbit

5. Partner Pass

One player sets up in center court position. From a nearby position, the partner drops and strokes a cross-court passing shot; the shot should hit the side wall high enough and hard enough to get an angled rebound from the back wall. The first player attempts to play the ball off the back wall. Players alternate positions after five attempts. Repeat twice. Try to remember the four principles of playing the back wall. Turn with the ball, keeping your eyes on it. Take the inside route, pivoting like a basketball player. Wait for the ball to drop. Try to plan what type of shot to return. Be sure to include some shots that require you and your partner to use the backhand.

Success Goal = 6 out of 10 playable shots returned

Your Score = (#) _____ out of 10 playable shots returned

6. *Partner Continuous Back Wall Setup*

Partners set each other up off the back wall. You can mix straight front-to-back or side-wall angled rebounds as desired. Keep the ball high enough so your partner can play it off the back wall.

Success Goal = 10 continuous back wall returns

Your Score = (#) _____ continuous back wall returns

7. *The Back Wall Game*

In this game, the only way to score is by returning a shot off the back wall that your opponent cannot return. Players start each rally with a serve and alternate serves regardless of who wins the rally. Try to hit passing shots and ceiling shots off the back wall to win the rally and score a point. The first player to get seven points wins the game. Know where your opponent is, and plan what shot to hit. Move with your shot, then move quickly toward center court and anticipate a return. Don't look back.

Success Goal = Win 2 out of 3 games

Your Score = (#) _____ games won

Back Wall Play
Keys to Success Checklist

Repeat Drill 6 and ask a trained observer to evaluate your ability to play the ball off the back wall according to the guidelines in Figure 11.5.

Step 12 Kill Shots

A kill shot is an offensive shot used to end a rally. It can be further defined as a shot hit so low on the front wall that it is impossible to return. With an effective kill shot you can score points or take the serve away from an opponent. The ultimate kill shot hits the front wall and the floor at the same time and does not bounce. This is called a *rollout*.

WHY ARE KILL SHOTS IMPORTANT?

Without an effective kill shot you would never be able to develop beyond a mediocre level. You must be able to take advantage of openings your opponent leaves for you. If you continue to hit all defensive shots, sooner or later you will leave an opening for your opponent. It can be good strategy to run your opponents in order to fatigue them, but you also must be able to put the point away when given the chance. The kill shot is the only shot that enables you to do that.

HOW TO EXECUTE THE KILL SHOTS

There are four different types of kill shots. The first three types are very similar: the straight (front wall only) kill, the pinch, and the inside corner kill. The fourth type is the drop (volley) kill. Each will be described separately, but all have many things in common. The novice tries to hit the kill shot very hard. This can be effective, but the shot must also be hit very low. It must be contacted low and must hit the front wall low. If it does not, power will actually make it a poorer shot, as it will rebound higher and be easier to handle.

Remember the laws of physics. If a ball is traveling at a downward angle, it will rebound upward at an equal angle. Therefore, on all but the fly kill, you must contact the ball lower than your knee. At ankle height is better. To do this, you must have excellent position on the ball. Better players ''wait'' for the ball to drop, then move into the shot.

The swing changes from an upright plane to more of a sidearm stroke in most instances. Remember the angle of the face of the racquet. The face should be square in the side-view plane to keep the ball and the rebound low. There is not much margin for error if you want to hit a good kill shot. The sidearm stroke increases that margin for error. To do this you must bend and move your body in a low, sideward manner. The exception to this would be a backhand kill. Even better players hit the backhand kill with an upright swing. It is easier to get the proper wrist cock from this position. The trade-off is that you must be very careful to be in good position and have the proper angle on the racquet face.

Do not overswing. Make sure the ball is hit low and stays low. The effective kill shot bounces twice before it gets back to the service line. If you can keep it that low, you will have a winner. Other kill shots may score points, but this one is guaranteed. The kill shot is most effective when your opponent is behind you. The novice should never try a kill shot when in the backcourt or the deep part of the midcourt. You should seldom try a kill shot when your opponent is in front of you. Better players can occasionally get by with it, but they also realize they are inviting a kill shot in return if they don't hit a great one. This is why it is so important to establish center court position before attempting a kill shot (remember Rule #2, ''I Own Center Court'').

STRAIGHT (FRONT WALL) KILL

The straight (front wall) kill is just a refinement of a good passing shot. In fact, many mediocre kill shots turn into effective down-the-line passing shots when kept near the side wall (see Figure 12.1). Be patient and let the ball drop low. Bend sideways and move with the stroke. Do not overswing. Keep your eye on the ball. Remember: Low is better than hard. Your target should be 2 to 6 inches above the

Figure 12.1 Effective straight kill shot.

Figure 12.2 Effective pinch kill shot.

floor on the front wall. Try to contact the ball at the same height from the floor.

PINCH KILL

The pinch kill is hit in much the same way as the straight kill except that the shot contacts the side wall about a foot from the front wall, then contacts the front wall. Some players refer to it as an outside corner kill shot. It should contact the sidewall 2 to 6 inches above the floor. Hitting two walls deadens the shot more than the straight kill. It also changes the angle of the rebound. The shot will tend to stay up front, making a return more difficult. This is an excellent kill shot to hit when your opponent is in the backcourt and on the same side of the court as the corner you hit (see Figure 12.2). It is much easier to keep low than the straight kill and has a greater chance for success. The best target for a right-handed player is the right corner and vice versa for the lefty.

INSIDE CORNER KILL

The inside corner kill is much like the pinch shot except that the ball contacts the front wall before the side wall. For this shot to be effective, the ball should hit the front wall near the

side wall—within 6 to 12 inches, depending upon the angle from which it is hit. The shot rebounds farther back than the pinch shot, but not as far back as the straight kill. The best target for a right-handed player is the left front corner and vice versa for a lefty. Your opponent's position is more important, however. If she or he is on one side of the midline, a kill shot to that corner is the most effective (see Figure 12.3). This also helps you decide whether to use a pinch or an inside corner kill shot.

Figure 12.4 summarizes the Keys to Success for executing three types of kill shots.

Figure 12.3 Effective inside corner kill shot.

Figure 12.4 Keys to Success: Three Kill Shots

Preparation Phase

1. Establish center court position ____
2. Opponent behind you ____
3. Wait for ball to drop ____
4. Eyes on ball ____
5. Visualize target
   a. Low on front wall for straight kill ____
   b. Front wall near corner for inside corner kill ____
   c. Side wall near corner for pinch ____
6. Front shoulder points
   a. To front wall for straight kill ____
   b. Toward corner for other kills ____

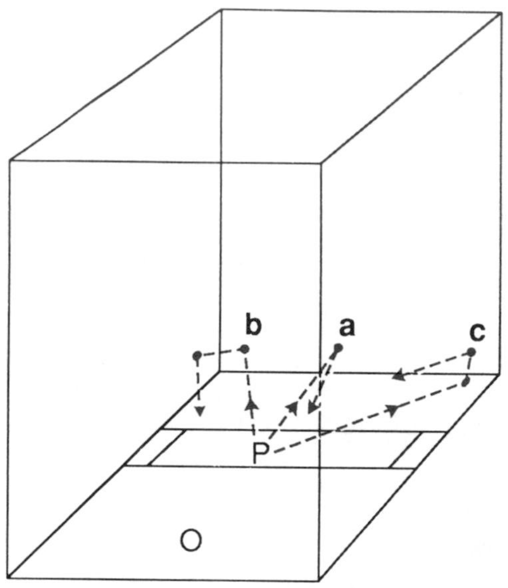

Execution Phase

1. Sidearm swing for forehand kill ____
2. Body low—move sideways ____
3. Transfer weight forward ____
4. Swing stays low—controlled ____
5. Move toward
   a. Front wall for straight kill ____
   b. Corner for inside corner kill ____
   c. Corner for pinch ____

Follow-Through Phase

1. Eyes and head still ____
2. Try to "see" racquet hit ball ____
3. Arm comes across— squares body ____
4. Gather balance—ready to move ____

DROP (VOLLEY) KILL

The drop or volley kill shot is contacted on the fly or before it bounces. It is used when your opponent is deep in the rear court and you can hit the ball in midcourt to surprise your opponent instead of allowing the ball to go to the back wall. Unlike in the other kill shots, you contact this shot above the knees—sometimes as high as the shoulders. Because of this, you must hit a soft shot to make it die in the corner. This is very similar to the drop shot in tennis. You open the racquet face and "cut" or "slice" the shot—in other words, put backspin on the ball. If you can deaden the ball enough, you do not have to cut it. Because the shot must be so soft, it must hit the side wall very close to the corner—within a few inches. The most effective drop kill hits the side wall first (see Figure 12.5).

It is difficult to set up a drill for the drop kill. The fundamentals are not much diffrent from the pinch and inside corner kills. The secret to success is catching your opponent by surprise and hitting the ball softly so a return is not possible.

Figure 12.5 Keys to Success: Drop Kill

Preparation Phase

1. Good position in front court—opponent very deep ____
2. Ball comes to you ____
3. Can be hit with any grip ____
4. Turn toward target corner ____
5. Short backswing—open racquet face ____
6. Disguise the shot as long as possible ____

Execution Phase

1. Visualize target
   a. Low in corner ____
   b. To either wall ____
2. "Catch" the ball on the strings ____
3. "Slice" the ball on the strings ____
4. Shorter swing—almost no swing ____

Follow-Through Phase

1. No follow-through with racquet ____
2. Do not drop back ____
3. Anticipate diving return by opponent ____
4. Be ready to put return away if it occurs ____

Detecting Kill Shot Errors

Kill shots require a lot of practice because they are very difficult to execute. Almost anyone can hit a hard shot low on the front wall, but to get it to bounce twice before the service line is very difficult. However, you must practice this if you are to improve as a racquetball player. The most difficult things to master are to let the ball drop very low and to bend your body low while transferring your weight forward. Check the following suggestions to improve your kill shot and the offensive part of your game.

ERROR 🚫

CORRECTION

1. Ball rebounds too far back from front wall.

2. Ball rebounds too high.

1. Don't swing as hard. Wait for the ball to drop before hitting it. Move with the ball while waiting for it to drop.

2. Ball should hit wall 2 to 6 inches high. Contact ball 2 to 6 inches from floor.

ERROR ⃠	CORRECTION
3. Ball "skips" (hits floor before front wall).	3. Transfer weight from rear to front foot—stay low. Follow through. Check your grip.
4. Opponent rekills your kill shots often.	4. Kill only when your opponent is behind you. Don't kill so often—use a low pass once in a while.

Kill Shot Drills

1. Paper Cup Kill

Place a ball on top of a paper cup near the midline and near the short serve line. If the mouth of the cup is too large, turn the cup upside-down. Practice straight wall, pinch, and inside corner kills with your forehand and backhand strokes. Remember to stay low and transfer your weight. Try to visualize your target low on the front wall and in the corners. Remember, to be effective, your kills must bounce twice before rebounding to the service line.

Success Goals = 5 effective kill shots using both forehand and backhand strokes for 3 different kill shots

Your Scores =

   a. (#) _____ effective forehand straight wall kills

   (#) _____ effective forehand pinch kills

   (#) _____ effective forehand inside corner kills

   b. (#) _____ effective backhand straight wall kills

   (#) _____ effective backhand pinch kills

   (#) _____ effective backhand inside corner kills

2. Kill From Midcourt

Standing in midcourt, toss the ball up and out in front of you. Move into the ball and hit kill shots with your forehand stroke. Hit straight, pinch, and inside corner kills. Next, use your backhand stroke for all three types of shots.

Success Goals = 5 effective kill shots using both forehand and backhand strokes for 3 different kill shots

Your Scores =

a. (#) ____ effective forehand kill shots

(#) ____ effective forehand pinch shots

(#) ____ effective forehand inside corner shots

b. (#) ____ effective backhand kill shots

(#) ____ effective backhand pinch shots

(#) ____ effective backhand inside corner shots

3. Kill From the Back Wall

Stand in the backcourt. Toss the ball against the back wall. Catch up with the ball on any bounce and hit a straight wall kill. Remember to stay low and move with the stroke. Try to keep it near a side wall. Next, repeat the drill using your backhand stroke. After that, drop the ball and hit it against the front wall high and hard enough to set yourself up off the back wall. Try to take it before it bounces a second time.

Success Goals = 3 effective straight wall kill shots (bounces twice before the service line) using both forehand and backhand strokes

Your Scores =

a. (#) ____ effective forehand straight wall kill shots from back wall toss

b. (#) ____ effective backhand straight wall kill shots from back wall toss

c. (#) ____ effective forehand straight wall kill shots from front wall setup

d. (#) ____ effective backhand straight wall kill shots from front wall setup

4. Kill From the Side Wall

Stand at midcourt about 3 feet from the side wall. Toss the ball softly up against the side wall. Move to position and hit straight, pinch, or inside corner kills with your forehand. Now, use the other wall and your backhand stroke.

Success Goals = 5 effective kill shots using both forehand and backhand strokes for 3 different kill shots

Your Scores =

a. (#) _____ effective forehand straight wall kills

 (#) _____ effective forehand pinch kills

 (#) _____ effective forehand inside corner kills

b. (#) _____ effective backhand straight wall kills

 (#) _____ effective backhand pinch kills

 (#) _____ effective backhand inside corner kills

5. *Partner Kill*

Partners rally a ball against the front wall so that the ball comes off the back wall into mid-court. After at least three hits, one tries to end the rally with a kill shot. The other tries to return it with another kill. Next, the partners hit ceiling shots until a poor ceiling shot ends up in center court. One player then tries a kill, and the other player attempts a rekill.

Success Goals = 5 out of 10 effective kill shots from back wall rally or ceiling shot that cannot be returned by partner

Your Scores

a. (#) _____ out of 10 effective kill shots from back wall rally

b. (#) _____ out of 10 effective kill shots from ceiling shot rally

6. *Five-Point Kill Game*

One player serves as in a game. Both players hit shots that will gain them center court position. Each looks for a kill opportunity. Any type of kill shot may be used. Only kill shots during play will win points. Errors or other shots during play can cause change of serve or end the rally, but will not score a point.

Success Goal = Win 2 out of 3 five-point kill games

Your Score = (#) _____ five-point kill games won

The kill shots are the last of the basic playing shots you will learn. They are what aggressive players live for. It is very satisfying to end a rally with a shot your opponent cannot return. The rollout is the epitome of kill shots, similar to a smash in tennis.

If the ball can be played anywhere near the midline, you should position yourself to play the kill shot with your forehand. You will hit much better kills with your forehand. In tennis, it is considered an error to run around your backhand to play the ball with a forehand stroke, but you can do this much more in racquetball without getting yourself in trouble. If you have good agility and court sense, you can run around your backhand without leaving an opening for your opponent. You will learn by experience how often to do this. The benefit of getting a much better kill shot is often worth the risk of leaving an opening.

Ask your instructor or a friend to watch you as you attempt the various kill shots. Have them use the Keys to Success in Figures 12.4 and 12.5 to help in the evaluation.

Step 13   Strategy Rule #4—
Stay Out of the Detour Zone

You learned in Step 5 about hitting the ball to your opponent's backhand. If you are doing that, you are probably winning your share of games. Next you learned how to control center court and play the back wall. Now you need to start improving the quality of your shots. This step will help you start planning and hitting better quality shots.

The detour zone is the center area of the front wall (see Figure 13.1). Shots returned to this area are not usually effective, especially at higher levels of play. If you could draw a line near the outside edges of the front wall, the border outside the line is the area you want your shots to contact. For beginners, this border would be about 3 to 4 feet wide. As you get better, the border should shrink accordingly. Look at the front wall of your court. Unless it has been recently painted, it is proba-

bly worn more in the detour zone than around the edges. Avoid this detour zone to win points!

WHY IS STRATEGY RULE #4 IMPORTANT?

Avoiding the detour zone will help you hit shots that are more difficult for your opponent to return. All players who learn racquetball start out by just trying to return the ball to the front wall. This rule will help you reach the next level of play. Your focus will shift to planning what type of shot to hit. When you reach this level of strategy, your level of play improves much faster.

HOW TO EXECUTE STRATEGY RULE #4

By this time you should have confidence that you can return most shots to the front wall. As you are getting into position for your shot, wait a little longer for the ball to drop lower to the floor before hitting it. As you are waiting, be aware of your opponent's court position. You can gather this information in several ways. You know where your opponent had to go to return your shot and how much time has passed since the return. Listen for any sounds of movement from your opponent. All this takes only a split second, yet it can be valuable in planning your shot. Now plan your shot to take advantage of any opening your opponent may have left. Try to visualize the border of the front wall that will be your target area. Concentrate on hitting your shot within this border. As you get better, try to reduce the width of the border.

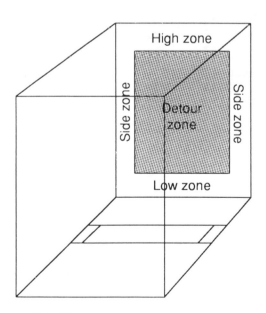

Figure 13.1 Detour zone.

Detecting Errors in Using Strategy Rule #4

When you are first learning the game, you don't have time to think about where your shot will go. Now that you have a little more confidence that you can return the ball, you can improve the quality of your shots. An observer can tell you things about yourself that you can't get on your own.

ERROR 🚫

CORRECTION

ERROR	CORRECTION
1. Many shots hit in detour zone.	1. Take more time for your shot. Let it drop or come away from the wall more. Don't swing so hard. Think about control more than power. Be patient. Recognizing that your shot hit in the detour zone is the first step in improving your shots.
2. Too many things to think about all at one time.	2. Concentrate first on visualizing the border and controlling the ball. The rest will come with more confidence.
3. General inconsistency.	3. Don't try to make perfect shots too soon. It takes years of playing and practice before your border shrinks to less than 1 foot.

Detour Zone Drills

You can drill for this rule any time just by being aware of where your ball strikes the front wall. This should include warm-up and serving.

1. Avoid the Detour Zone

With tape or colored chalk, mark a 3- or 4-foot border on the front wall. If you don't have a ladder, just mark the low border and the side borders as high as you can reach. Warm up and hit practice shots with a partner trying to "Stay Out of the Detour Zone." Remember to remove the tape or chalk lines when you are done using the court.

Success Goal = 5 minutes of practice hitting shots

Your Score = (#) _____ minutes practicing with marked border

2. Detour Zone Game

Use a court marked as in previous drill. Play 3 games to five points with an opponent. Only shots hit into the border score a point. Serve alternates as in regular game, but may not result in a point. Shots hit by a receiver can win a point as well as those by the server.

Success Goal = Win 2 of 3 five-point games

Your Score = (#) _____ five-point games

3. Detour Zone Chart

Use court unmarked or marked as previously described. Play a game to seven points. Ask a third person to chart your shots (see your instructor for a form or make your own similar to Figure 13.2). Be sure to tell your observer the width of your border—3 or 4 feet is recommended for beginners. Mark shots with an X where they hit the front wall. Circle the X if the shot ends the rally. Calculate the percentage of shots that hit in the high zone, low zone, side zones, and detour zone. Analyze your results.

Ask someone to chart your shots as often as you can. The knowledge that someone is charting your shots will help you to concentrate on your target areas. If you do this often, the quality of your shots will improve rapidly.

Success Goal = More than 60 percent of shots out of detour zone

Your Score = (%) _____ shots out of detour zone

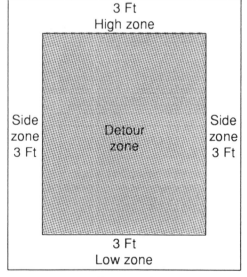

Figure 13.2 Detour zone chart.

Step 14   Cutthroat—For Fun and Improvement

Cutthroat is an unofficial game that is played at all levels. The game is played with three people. The server always plays a singles game against two opponents who are a doubles team.

WHY IS CUTTHROAT IMPORTANT?

This game makes it more difficult for the server to score points. Two players playing as a team can cover the court better than a single player. This forces the server to hit better quality shots to win the rally and score a point. Cutthroat also neutralizes the server's natural advantage on the serve, which is especially pronounced at the novice level. The partner returning the serve is better able to concentrate on the return, knowing that the other partner can move to cover any opening created.

Advanced players like to play cutthroat because they feel it improves their offensive shots. It also works out well when there are three players and all wish to play.

HOW TO PLAY CUTTHROAT

Each player keeps her or his own score. Most games are played until one player has 15 or 21 points. Because it is an unofficial game, tournaments are never held, and you can set the winning score wherever you wish. Play continues until the server loses the serve. Players then rotate clockwise. The new server serves to the new doubles team formed by the ex-server and the third player. The rotation of servers continues after each loss of serve until one player reaches the score agreed upon. There are no rules regarding placement of serves, but for fun and sportsmanship, many players alternate serves to the two receivers. For the doubles team, either partner may play the ball and all other doubles rules apply to them. The most important of the doubles rules are as follows:

- One cannot call a hinder on one's partner.
- If one returns the ball toward the front wall and it strikes one's partner, it is loss of the rally.
- If one partner swings and misses, the other may legally return the ball as long as it is in play.

Side-by-Side Style

When you are partners with someone, you must decide what style of play or what positions you will use. The side-by-side style (Figure 14.1) should be used for receiving serves and any time the server has the offensive. It can also be used all the time during play. There are strong points and weak points with this style of play.

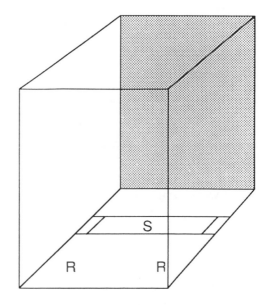

Figure 14.1 Side-by-side formation.

Strong Points: Side-by-Side Style

- You start in this position, so no changes are necessary.
- Both players can easily keep contact with each other.
- It is hard for the singles player to pass you. You can make the server run by using passing shots.
- Stronger players can help weaker players by covering more of the court.
- One player's backhand can be protected.

Weak Points: Side-by-Side Style

- The singles player can hit more kill shots. This style is not as strong defensively on the front wall.
- Both players must move up and back together, or else a weakness will be created.
- Players must communicate closely.
- Shots that go between the players might lead to confusion. The player with the forehand shot should always make the return.

Up-and-Back Style

The up-and-back style (Figure 14.2), also called the *I formation*, is sometimes used by players after receiving the serve. When the partners hit a shot that takes the singles player out of center court, one player can assume the center court position slightly closer to the front wall than in singles. The other player then stays in the deep center court position. The front player takes any shots he or she wishes, including volleys. The other player takes any shots that get past the ''up'' player. The more aggressive player makes a good up player, whereas the retriever with a good backhand makes the ideal back player.

Strong Points: Up-and-Back Style

- Can kill any weak returns by the singles player.
- Eliminates doubt as to which player takes which shot.

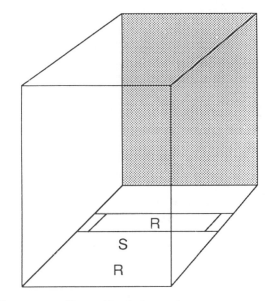

Figure 14.2 Up-and-back formation.

- Can run the singles player front to back easily.
- Can put players in positions they like to play.

Weak Points: Up-and-Back Style

- Singles player can more easily work on and isolate the weaker player.
- Down-the-line kills and passes are effective against this formation.
- The front player cannot see where her or his partner is, and sometimes has difficulty deciding when to let shots go by.
- Hard shots right at the front player are hard to handle.

Serving and Playing Singles in Cutthroat

You must remember that there are two players against you. This means you must change your game and the type of shots you use. You no longer can run an opponent with shot selections. Your kill shots must be better because one player can take more chances while the partner covers. If the partners are playing side by side, try the following:

- Use kill shots if you are in front of them.
- Do not pass, especially down the line.

- If you do pass, use a high cross-court pass.
- Around-the-wall shots and Z-shots may work well if the doubles players don't communicate well (see Step 17 for these shots).
- Occasionally hit the ball down the center of the court—between them.
- Work on the weaker player.

If they are playing up and back, try these:

- Down-the-line passing shots and cross-court passes are good.

- Do not try to kill if the front player is in front of you.
- Hit the ball hard so the front player has less time to react. Sometimes a ball at the front player is effective.
- Ceiling shots to the backhand of the deep player can give you time to recover.
- Work on the weaker player.

Cutthroat Drill

Cutthroat Game

Play four games of cutthroat. Set the winning score at seven points. Change the order of rotation after each game so you don't serve to the same person's backhand all the time. If you have four players, either the server rotates out of the court after the loss of serve or one player sits out one game. This fourth player could chart detour-zone shots.

Success Goal = Play 4 games to seven points

Your Score = (#) _____ games played

Step 15 Z-Serves

The Z-serves get their name from the path they follow around the court. They are served into the corner from near the opposite side wall. There are two types: the hard Z-serve, which imparts spin (''English'') on the ball so it comes off the opposite wall at an unusual angle, and the soft Z-serve, which should die in the opposite back corner. Both are thought of as change-ups from the power serve and the lob serve.

WHY ARE THE Z-SERVES IMPORTANT?

Any serve is important because it is the start of the way you can win a point. The Z-serves give the receiver different angles and speeds to adjust to. Too often the power player continues to serve the same serve time after time, and the receiver simply adjusts to that single serve, just as a batter can adjust to a power pitcher who throws the baseball the same way every time.

HOW TO EXECUTE THE Z-SERVES

Both serves are more effective when served to the receiver's backhand. If both the server and the receiver are right-handed, the hard Z-serve is more difficult to execute, but it is still worth learning. Any other combination of right-handed server and left-handed receiver, or vice versa, just makes the serve much more effective.

The Hard Z-Serve

Assuming that you and your receiver are both right-handed, start to the left of center within the serving area. Move toward the opposite corner as if serving a power serve. Drop the ball a little closer to your body than for the power serve. The ball should be struck hard and hit the front wall approximately 1 foot from the corner. Rotate your wrist and elbow out slightly to open your racquet face. Your stroke should be more underhand than sidearm. A right-handed player serving to the left corner or a left-handed player serving to the right corner would use a normal sidearm swing. The ball contacts the sidewall and comes across the court bouncing on the floor close to the opposite side wall. If the ball is struck hard enough initially, it will then rebound from the side wall at an unnatural angle. It will squeak when it hits the floor and side wall and rebound perpendicular to the side wall. This causes adjustment problems for the receiver, especially if the serve is deep in the court when it strikes the side wall. Ideally, the ball will rebound parallel to the back wall and only 2 or 3 feet from it (see Figure 15.1, a and b). Varying the power and point of contact in the corner gives an infinite number of return adjustments to the receiver. Because you are taking yourself out of position to gain the proper angle into the corner, you must concentrate on moving across and back to center court as quickly as possible. Do not watch the ball after it has passed the service area. Assume the ready position and anticipate the return of the ball by your opponent. Figure 15.2, a-e, shows the technique Keys to Success for executing the hard Z-serve.

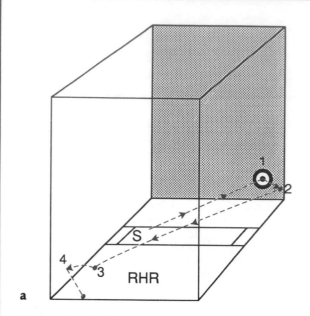
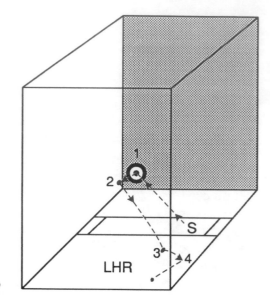

Figure 15.1 Ball path for hard Z-serves to right-handed receiver (a) and to left-handed receiver (b).

Figure 15.2 Keys to Success: Hard Z-Serve

Preparation Phase

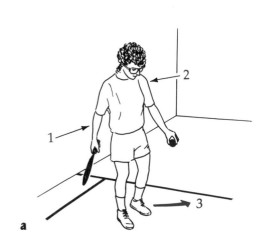
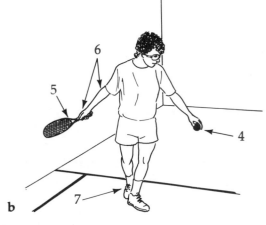

1. Start from near side wall ____
2. Nonracquet shoulder pointing toward corner ____
3. Movement is diagonal toward corner ____

4. Drop ball toward corner ____
5. Backswing almost behind body ____
6. Elbow and wrist rotate ____
7. Start serve with rear crossover step ____

Execution
Phase

c

d

1. Front foot steps toward corner ____
2. Weight shifts to front foot ____
3. Arm swing is nearly vertical ____

4. Arm passes close to leg ____
5. Swing toward target corner ____
6. Eyes on ball ____

Follow-Through
Phase

1. Rear foot forward and out ____
2. Quickly regain balance ____
3. Drop back to center court position ____
4. Assume ready position ____
5. Anticipate receiver's return ____
6. Do not look back ____

e

The Soft Z-Serve

The soft Z-serve, sometimes called a *high Z-serve*, is struck similarly to the lob serve. An overhand stroke is recommended. Stand left of center in the serving area (right-hander serving to right-hander). Face the right-hand corner. Bounce the ball on the floor in front of your right shoulder. Hit the ball so it strikes the front wall about 2 feet from the corner and 3 to 4 feet below the ceiling. This will give the same Z pattern to the opposite wall, but the ball will not "Z" off the wall. It should bounce high into the rear corner and fall sharply, dying into the corner (see Figure 15.3, a and b). As with the hard Z-serve, the server must hustle into position for the receiver's return. Figure 15.4, a-e, shows the technique Keys to Success for executing the soft Z-serve.

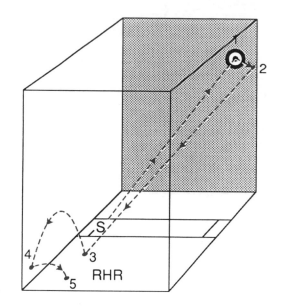
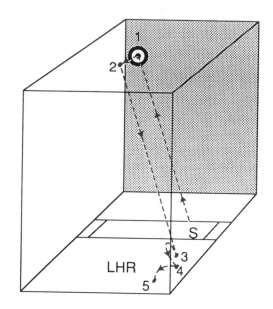

Figure 15.3 Ball path for soft Z-serves to right-handed receiver (a) and to left-handed receiver (b).

Figure 15.4 Keys to Success:
Soft Z-Serve

**Preparation
Phase**

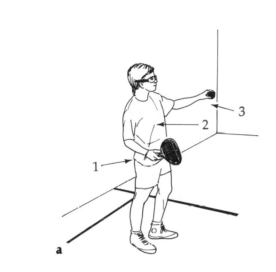 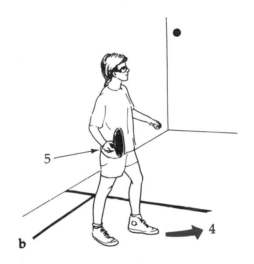

1. Start from near side
   wall ____
2. Face target corner
   squarely ____
3. Bounce ball out in
   front ____

4. Step toward ball with
   nonracquet foot ____
5. Racquet back behind
   shoulder ____

Execution
Phase

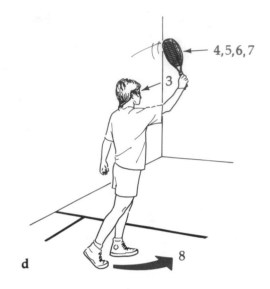

1. Push off rear foot ____
2. Shift weight to front foot ____
3. Eyes on ball ____
4. Racquet face square to corner ____
5. Aim for spot high on front wall____

6. Hit ball softly but firmly ____
7. Racquet points toward corner ____
8. Rear foot comes forward and out ____

Follow-Through
Phase

1. Follow-through shortened ____
2. Do not watch ball ____
3. Move quickly to center court ____
4. Assume ready position ____
5. Do not look back ____
6. Look for kill opportunity ____

RETURNING Z-SERVES

Both the hard Z-serve and the soft Z-serve can be difficult to return. It is important to be patient and stroke the return rather than lunge at it. Both serves are change-ups, and you must not let yourself rush your return. The situation is very similar to a baseball batter trying to hit a change-up from the pitcher. Watch the ball carefully, plan your return shot, then smoothly execute the shot. The following sections will give you some more specific pointers.

Hard Z-Serve Return

This serve is hit hard, but after it "Zs" off the side wall it is actually traveling slowly. If you realize this, you shouldn't panic or rush your return. You probably can't cut the serve off before it crosses the court and bounces against the side wall. Your first move should be to a point exactly even with where the ball will "Z" off the side wall and on the opposite side of the imaginary midline (see Figure 15.5). Watch the ball the entire time you are moving and then turn to face the ball coming off the side wall. It is important to stay away from the ball. How far on the opposite side of the midline you set up depends on how far you expect the ball to rebound. You can always move forward faster than you can backward. If you are not on the opposite side of the midline, the ball will be too close to you and will "handcuff" you, or restrict your arm extension and swing. The safest return will be a ceiling shot to the server's backhand corner. Another good possiblity is a down-the-line pass along the side wall the server just vacated. This assumes the Z-serve has been hit to your backhand side. The server should never serve to your forehand, but if she or he makes that mistake, a down-the-line pass would be your first choice.

Soft Z-Serve Return

This serve is very difficult to return if you let it get to the rear corner. Your first option should be to cut it off before it bounces on the

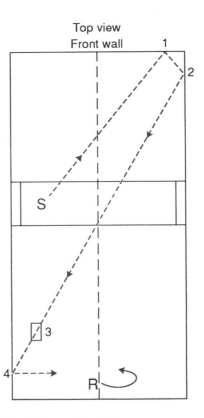

Figure 15.5 Return of hard Z-serve.

floor. It will probably be close to the floor before you can get to it, so you will want to hit a cross-court pass or down-the-line pass. This depends upon where the server is and where you must contact the ball. You might also try a pinch kill shot. This maneuver frequently takes the server by surprise and can end the rally. This return is much easier to execute if you can use your forehand stroke. You also have the option to let the serve come to the backcourt. If the ball has been struck too hard or too softly, this is a good option. Experience can tell you when to cut the serve off and when to let it come to the backcourt. If you do let it come to the backcourt, you should hit a defensive shot. The server will have had time to move to the center court position, so consider a ceiling shot to the backhand corner as your first choice. A passing shot would be your second option. Figure 15.6 provides a summary of the key points for both the server and receiver of Z-serves.

Hard Z-Serve (Right- or left-handed server)	Soft Z-Serve (Right- or left-handed server)
For right-handed receivers:	**For right-handed receivers:**
Serve from near left side wall. **Target**—right corner. **First bounce**—15-18 feet behind short serve line. 2-3 feet from the left side wall. **Second bounce**—15-18 feet behind short line. 3-8 feet from left side wall. **Receiver position**—normal. **Receiver moves to**—face left side wall and opposite where ball will hit the wall. Stay back from the side wall on opposite side of midline. Passing or ceiling shot return.	Serve from near left side wall. **Target**—right corner 3-4 feet below ceiling and 2 feet from side wall. **First bounce**—5 feet behind short serve line. 4-5 feet from opposite (left) side wall. **Second bounce**—Very near left rear corner. **Receiver position**—normal. **Receiver moves to**—First choice: cut off serve on fly as it crosses the court (near midline). Pinch kill or passing shot. Second choice: hit return soon after first bounce. Ceiling shot return.
For left-handed receivers:	**For left-handed receivers:**
Serve from near right side wall. **Target**—left corner. **First bounce**: 15-18 feet behind short serve line and 2-3 feet from right side wall. **Second bounce**: 15-18 feet behind short serve line and 3-8 feet from right side wall. **Receiver position**—normal. **Receiver moves to**—face right side wall and opposite where ball will hit the wall. Stay back from side wall on opposite side of midline. Passing or ceiling shot return.	Serve from near right side wall. **Target**—left corner 3-4 feet below ceiling and 2 feet from side wall. **First bounce**: 5 feet behind short serve line and 4-5 feet from opposite (right) side wall. **Second bounce**: Very near right rear corner. **Receiver position**—normal. **Receiver moves to**—First choice: cut off serve on fly as it crosses the court (near midline). Pinch kill or passing shot. Second choice: hit return soon after first bounce. Ceiling shot return.

Figure 15.6 Z-serve summary chart.

Detecting Errors in the Z-Serves

The hard Z-serve is a difficult one to execute. Usually the problem is lack of power. The server must move in the proper direction to generate enough power. Do not get discouraged. Keep trying and you will eventually have a valuable serve. The soft Z-serve is much easier to learn. The drills will help you improve both serves.

ERROR ⊘	CORRECTION
1. Hard Z-serve does not ''Z'' off side wall.	1. Serve must be hit hard. Keep working on your power. Move your body toward the corner when serving. Use an upright swing with racquet close to body.
2. Hard Z-serve lands in front of short serve line.	2. Serve must hit in corner 3 to 4 feet high. Serve must be hit hard.
3. Hard Z-serve has correct action but is not deep enough.	3. Ball must contact front wall farther from corner. Server is too close to side wall when contacting serve. Start serve closer to midline of court. Experiment with different starting positions.
4. Soft Z-serve does not get deep enough.	4. Serve should contact wall farther from corner. The correct distance is 2 to 4 feet, depending upon the server's position. Serve from a position closer to the midline of the service area. The serve should strike the front wall within 3 or 4 feet of the ceiling.
5. Soft Z-serve rebounds out into court for easy return.	5. Serve must be hit softly so it dies in corner.

Z-Serve Drills

1. Dry Run—Hard Z-Serves

Without a ball, go through the motions of the hard Z-serve. It is important to do the cross-over step with the rear foot and still maintain a diagonal direction toward the opposite corner. Have partner give tips on movement and arm swing. Change with partner after five turns. Repeat twice.

Success Goal = 10 dry-run hard Z-serves

Your Score = (#) _____ dry-run hard Z-serves

2. Dry Run—Soft Z-Serves

Without a ball, go through the motions of the soft Z-serve. Remember to step toward the corner and square the racquet face toward the corner. The partner observes this and also checks the swing velocity. Give advice if the swing is too hard or too soft. Change with your partner after five turns. Repeat the swing twice.

Success Goal = 10 dry-run soft Z-serves

Your Score = (#) _____ dry-run soft Z-serves

3. Hard Z-Serve

Do this with a partner. The server serves a hard Z-serve. Both observe where the service contacts the front wall and the side wall in the corner—follow the action of the ball. Compare observations on angles, depth of serve, and direction of movement of the server while serving. Use Figure 15.1 to refresh your memory. Experiment with different angles to try to get serve deep in the court. Change with your partner after five serves. Repeat twice.

Success Goal = 10 hard Z-serves

Your Score = (#) _____ hard Z-serves

4. Soft Z-Serve With Partner

The server serves a soft Z-serve. Both observe where the serve contacts the front wall (3 to 4 feet below the ceiling and 2 feet from the corner) and the side wall in the corner. Follow the action of the ball. It should die in the opposite back corner. Compare observations on angle, velocity, depth of serve, and direction of movement of the server during the serve (refer to Figure 15.3). Move your starting position if the serve does not produce the desired results. Change with your partner after five serves. Repeat twice.

Success Goal = 10 soft Z-serves

Your Score = (#) _____ soft Z-serves

5. *Hard Z-Serves With Receiver Catch*

The server serves a hard Z-serve. The receiver has no racquet and tries to catch the ball as it rebounds from the second side wall. The receiver remembers to move from the receiving position to a spot exactly even with where the ball will contact the side wall. She or he faces the side wall and stands on the opposite side of the midline (see Figure 15.5). Distance depends upon the velocity of the serve. If the serve is not hard enough, the receiver must adjust position. The server concentrates on moving toward the center court position and not watching receiver.

Success Goal = Receiver catches 7 of 10 hard Z-serves

Your Score = (#) _____ caught of 10 hard Z-serves

6. *Soft Z-Serves With Receiver Catch*

The server serves a soft Z-serve. The receiver has no racquet and tries to catch the ball as it crosses the midline and before it hits the floor. The receiver should start from the normal receiving position. First attempt to catch 10 soft Z-serves before they strike the floor. Then let the serve go to the back corner. Attempt to catch 10 serves before the second bounce.

Success Goals =
   a. Receiver catches 7 of 10 soft Z-serves before first bounce
   b. Receiver catches 7 of 10 soft Z-serves between first and second bounces

Your Scores =
   a. (#) _____ caught before first bounce
   b. (#) _____ caught between first and second bounces

7. *Return of Hard Z-Serve by Receiver With Observer*

The server serves a hard Z-serve. The receiver tries to return it with a ceiling shot or a passing shot. The server moves quickly to the center court position and anticipates the return. The server tries to move to catch the return between the racquet and hand. The observer notes the server's movement to center court and the quality of his or her ready position. After five serves, rotate to different tasks. Repeat the cycle twice.

Success Goals =

a. 7 of 10 successful returns of hard Z-serve by receiver

b. 10 returns to center court position by server

Your Scores =

a. (#) _____ successful returns by receiver

b. (#) _____ times returned to center court by server

8. Return of Soft Z-Serve by Receiver With Observer

The server serves a soft Z-serve. The receiver tries to return it before the first bounce. Right-handed receivers should run around their backhand to make the shot with their forehand if the ball is anywhere near the midline. The receiver tries to return with a passing shot or a pinch kill shot. The server moves quickly to the center court position, sets up in the ready position, and attempts to trap the return between the racquet and hand. The observer notes the server's movement to center court and the quality of her or his ready position. After five serves, rotate to different tasks. Repeat the cycle twice. Next, repeat the drill with the receiver attempting to return the serve between the first and second bounces. Try to return with a ceiling shot.

Success Goals =

a. 7 out of 10 successful returns of soft Z-serve by receiver before the first bounce

b. 7 out of 10 successful returns of soft Z-serve by receiver between first and second bounces

c. 10 returns to center court position by server (each time) 20 total

Your Scores =

a. (#) _____ successful returns by receiver (before first bounce)

b. (#) _____ successful returns by receiver (between first and second bounces)

c. (#) _____ times returned to center court by server

9. Z-Serve Game

Play a game to seven points with an opponent. Alternate turns at service regardless of who wins the point. Use only soft Z-serves. The server gets one point if the receiver fails to make a legal return. The receiver gets one point for a legal return of the service. Servers do not play the return. Play three games. Then, using the same rules, play three games using the hard Z-serve.

Success Goals =

    a. Win 2 out of 3 soft Z-serve games

    b. Win 2 out of 3 hard Z-serve games

Your Scores =

    a. (#) _____ soft Z-serve games won

    b. (#) _____ hard Z-serve games won

Z-Serves
Keys to Success Checklists

Now ask a friend or your instructor to use the Keys to Success Checklists in Figures 15.2 and 15.4 and the summary chart in Figure 15.6 to evaluate your Z-serves. You now have all the serves you need to keep a receiver off-balance. Practice all of them and use a variety of serves when playing your games. You will be pleasantly surprised at the effectiveness of this tactic. The softer serves also help to keep your arm from getting tired, thus saving it for your kills and low passing shots. Variety is the spice of life, and varying the power and type of serves will make you a much better player.

Step 16 Strategy Rule #5— High–High, Low–Low

This rule is the next step in becoming a good racquetball player. It has several parts. The first is that if the ball comes to you high, return it high. A ceiling shot is the only shot you have at this point. In Step 17 you will develop another shot or two, but for now take comfort in the fact that the ceiling shot is very effective and difficult to return (especially from the backhand side).

The second part of Rule #5 itself has two parts. First, if the ball comes to you low, return it low. Two shots you could use for this are the kill shot and the low passing shot. Secondly, if you wish to return a shot low on the front wall and it is not low, you must wait for the ball to drop low before you hit it. This happens when a high returned ball such as a ceiling shot doesn't go back to the rear of the court. It could also occur when a ball rebounds high and hard from the back wall. If you want to hit a low shot such as a kill shot, wait for the ball to drop low, or the resulting shot will have a downward angle and the rebound will come back too high. This will present opportunities for your opponent to hit an effective kill shot in return.

This rule also relates closely to Strategy Rule #4, ''Stay Out of the Detour Zone.'' As you return a high ball, think of hitting high on the front wall—out of the detour zone. A low ball should be returned low—out of the detour zone.

WHY IS STRATEGY RULE #5 IMPORTANT?

Some people play a long time before they realize the significance of this concept. The ball will hit the front wall and then the floor, and then rebound at the same angle at which it contacted the front wall. So if you contact the ball higher than your waist, it will rebound from the front wall very high. Unless it is very close to the side wall, it will be an easy return for your opponent.

The other situation also creates weak returns. If the ball is contacted low and returned high, it will give an easy shot to your opponent. You often see players who dive for the ball in the front court do this. They will just get to a low ball with an open racquet face, and the open face will make the ball go up. This leads to a setup for the opponent. To try to hit a ceiling shot off a low ball also gives bad results. This ceiling shot has no chance to get deep in the court. Your opponent will likely let it drop low and kill it.

HOW TO EXECUTE STRATEGY RULE #5

You must think about your shots before you hit them. If you get into a hitting position early, you have more time to plan your shot. Decide quickly which type of shot and what angle to try. You won't always hit perfect shots, but without a goal you will just aimlessly return shots until your opponent gets the opportunity she or he is looking for. It will be much better for you to have a plan for each shot and work your plan until you have the opportunity you want.

Detecting Errors in Using Strategy Rule #5

As with other strategy rules, most problems that occur here are mental. Getting into position early and making your decision early will go a long way toward eliminating all the errors. A ceiling shot for high returns and a passing shot for low returns are usually high-percentage shots.

ERROR

CORRECTION

1. Low shots are easily handled by opponent.	1. Wait for the ball to drop lower. Don't try kill shots if opponent is not deep enough. Passing shots are better if opponent is even with you or in front of you.
2. Hard to decide whether to hit high shot or wait for low shot.	2. If opponent is in front of you, hit a high shot. If opponent stays back, hit a low shot. If opponent tries to deceive you and comes up late, hit a low passing shot.
3. General inconsistency or indecision.	3. Get there early and concentrate on the ball. If in doubt, hit a high (ceiling) shot.

"High–High, Low–Low" Drills

1. Ceiling Shot—Kill Shot

Start a ceiling shot rally with a partner. Wait for a ceiling shot that rebounds only to center court. Wait for the ball to drop, and execute any type of kill shot. The other player tries to return the kill shot with a low return. This should end the rally.

Success Goal = 5 repetitions of drill

Your Score = (#) _____ repetitions

2. Game Situation—Seven-Point Games

Play a game to seven points. Have an observer chart the number of balls you return from waist height or above. At this stage, you should return at least 80 percent of them with a high shot. Also have the observer record the number returned from below your waist. You should return at least 80 percent of them with a low shot.

Success Goals =

a. 80 percent of high balls returned high

b. 80 percent of low balls returned low

Your Scores =

a. (%) _____ of high balls returned high

b. (%) _____ of low balls returned low

Evaluation Checklist for Rule #5: "High–High, Low–Low"

As with most of the shots in reacquetball, getting into a hitting position early, plus making an early and good decision about what shot to hit, are essential if one wants to hit an effective shot. Ask your teacher or a friend to observe you as you play a game and give you this feedback. Use this evaluation checklist for the observation.

Preparation Phase

_____ Anticipates opponent's return of the shot—is in ready position and/or moving to center court.

_____ Watches ball closely while moving.

_____ Moves quickly into position to hit the ball. Does not time arrival to get there just in time, but gets there early and has time to set up for shot.

_____ Is aware of opponent's position. Seems to use peripheral vision, keeping eyes on ball, but still knows opponent's position.

Execution
Phase

____ Stays aware of position of opponent. Looks and/or listens for late movement.

____ Appears to be concentrating—presumably planning shot.

____ Ball is hit high or low, whatever is appropriate. High shots are high enough, low shots are low enough. All are outside of the imaginary detour zone.

Follow-Through
Phase

____ Player moves toward center court immediately. Does not stand and watch shot or opponent.

____ Player sets up in ready position at center court if there is enough time.

____ Player does not look back. Instead focuses on front wall and is alert and anticipating opponent's return.

Did your observer give you good marks on the evaluation checklist? If so, you are doing well and are ready to go on to the rest of the material. If not, analyze the areas you need to work on. Reviewing some earlier steps in the book may help.

Step 17 Z-Shot and Around-the-Wall Shot

The Z-shot is hit high into a corner on the front wall, striking the front wall first. It then travels across the court and strikes the other side wall. This causes the ball to "Z" straight out from the wall at a 90-degree angle. Any other type of shot would bounce off the side wall at an angle equal to the angle from which it approached. This Z, if deep enough in the court, will cause your opponent to retreat and hit a defensive shot.

The around-the-wall shot hits in the front corner but hits the side wall first. This shot has no "Z" effect, but it also causes your opponent to play the ball high or retreat to the backcourt to play it.

Note the difference between Z-shots and Z-serves. The serves must bounce on the floor before contacting the second side wall. The Z-shot executed during a rally travels directly from one side wall to the other.

WHY ARE THE Z-SHOT AND THE AROUND-THE-WALL SHOT IMPORTANT?

These shots are considered defensive shots. They are designed to drive your opponent out of the center court position and allow you time to get to center court. They are most often used when a shot draws you into the front court area and you wish to buy time to get back to the center court area. They are two of the best shots for this purpose.

HOW TO EXECUTE THE Z-SHOT

The Z-shot is executed like the hard Z-serve except that you hit the ball very high into the corner. It travels across the court and, unlike the hard Z-serve, should strike the opposite side wall before striking the floor (see Figure 17.1, a and b). This shot is most effective when returning a high ball from near a side wall. The shot can be hit with an overhead or sidearm swing from either the fore-

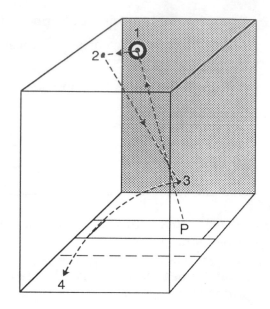

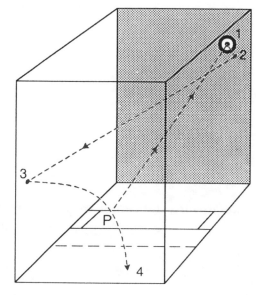

Figure 17.1 Z-shot to left (a) and right (b) front corners.

hand or the backhand side. Strike the ball hard so it hits the front wall first within 6 feet or less of the ceiling. The ball must be hit hard so it stays high as it crosses the court. The distance the ball hits from the side wall varies. If you are near the front wall, the ball should strike the wall 5 to 6 feet from the corner. The distance from the corner decreases as your position is deeper in the court. From a mid-court position the ball should strike within 2 feet of the corner. As soon as you hit the ball, move quickly toward center court.

HOW TO EXECUTE THE AROUND-THE-WALL SHOT

The around-the-wall shot hits the side wall first (see Figure 17.2, a and b). It is usually hit from near the front wall and a position near the midline. If your position is to the side of the midline, you should attempt a Z-shot into the opposite corner. The around-the-wall shot is hit high and hard like the Z-shot. The distance from the corner varies as with the Z-shot. The farther back you are in the court, the nearer to the corner the ball must hit. Both shots force your opponent to make a major adjustment. The bounce from these shots causes your opponent to play the ball while it is going from side wall to side wall. This is very different from the bounces from other types of shots. It almost forces your opponent to hit a defensive shot from these bounces. That is the secret of the effectiveness of these shots. The around-the-wall shot is not as effective as the Z-shot because the ball usually rebounds toward the center court area from the rear of the court. The Z-shot will usually remain deeper (nearer the back wall).

The following Keys to Success give you guidelines about when and how to use the Z-shot and around-the-wall shot effectively (see Figure 17.3).

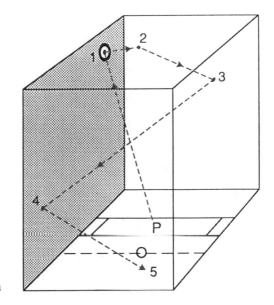

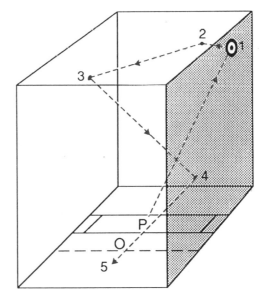

Figure 17.2 Around-the-wall shot to left (a) and right (b) front corners.

Figure 17.3 Keys to Success:
Z-Shot and Around-the-Wall Shot

**Preparation
Phase**

Z-Shot   **Around-the-Wall Shot**

____ 1. Ball is high and near front
court   ____

2. Ball on one side of   2. Ball near midline ____
midline ____

____ 3. Face target corner   ____

**Execution
Phase**

Z-Shot   **Around-the-Wall Shot**

____ 1. Overhead or sidearm stroke   ____
____ 2. Hit ball hard enough to stay
high as it crosses the court.
Forces opponent to retreat to
back court.   ____

3. Ball strikes front wall   3. Ball strikes side wall
high ____   high ____

4. Hit front wall first, 2 to   4. Hit side wall first, 2 to 6
6 feet from corner ____   feet from corner ____

____ 5. Ball stays high crossing court
and out of opponent's reach   ____

____ 6. Ball hits high on other side
wall   ____

**Follow-Through
Phase**

Z-Shot		Around-the-Wall Shot
____	1. Do not watch ball	____
____	2. Move quickly to center court	____
____	3. Set up in ready position	____
____	4. Anticipate lengthy wait for return	____
____	5. Do not look back	____

Detecting Errors in the Z-Shot and the Around-the-Wall Shot

These two shots are easy to learn and easy to execute. One of your biggest problems will be remembering to use them enough. They are not powerful offensive shots but will buy you time if you get pulled too far up front.

ERROR

CORRECTION

1. Shots do not get deep enough in the court.

2. The ball hits the ceiling and does not go deep enough in the court.

3. Opponent often hits the return on the fly and passes you.

1. The ball is hitting too close to the corner. Move your target farther from the corner.

2. Contact the ball when it is higher in the air. If that is not possible, try a kill shot or passing shot. You can also lower your target in the corner.

3. Be sure to keep the ball high enough.

Z-Shot and Around-the-Wall Shot Drills

1. Z-Shot

From a spot 4 to 6 feet from your forehand wall, bounce the ball high as for the lob serve. Hit a Z-shot into the opposite corner with your forehand stroke. Hit five from the service line and five from the short serve line. Hit closer to the corner as you move deeper in the court. Hit the ball high and hard, and watch the Z effect and resulting bounces. Repeat the same drill with your backhand stroke from the other side wall area.

Success Goals = 15 Z-shots with both forehand and backhand strokes from two different starting points

Your Scores =

   a. (#) _____ Z-shots with forehand stroke from service line

       (#) _____ Z-shots with forehand stroke from short serve line

   b. (#) _____ Z-shots with backhand stroke from service line

       (#) _____ Z-shots with backhand stroke from short serve line

2. Z-Shot and Return

One person hits a Z-shot as in Drill 1. The partner tries to return each Z-shot using a ceiling shot or passing shot. Use the same guidelines as in returning the hard Z-serve. The ball will rebound farther from the sideline across the midline. You might even have to let it rebound off the other side wall. The person who hit the Z-shot moves to center court and faces the front wall. Do not look back. Do not play the return.

Success Goals = 10 out of 15 Z-shots returned with both forehand and backhand strokes

Your Scores =

   a. (#) _____ forehand Z-shots returned

   b. (#) _____ backhand Z-shots returned

3. Around-the-Wall Shot

From a position near the midline, bounce the ball high as for a lob serve. Hit this shot into the corner, striking the side wall first. The ball should hit 2 to 6 feet from the corner, depending on your position in the court. Practice hitting five from the service line and five from the short serve line. Hit closer to the corner as you move deeper in the court. Hit the ball high and hard, and watch the bounces. Repeat the drill using your backhand stroke.

Success Goals = 15 around-the-wall shots with both forehand and backhand strokes

Your Scores =

a. (#) _____ around-the-wall shots forehand

b. (#) _____ around-the-wall shots backhand

4. Around-the-Wall Shot With Partner Return

Practice the around-the-wall shot drill with a partner. Start the drill as in Drill 3. Your partner should be in the center court position. Your partner tries to return each shot using a ceiling shot or passing shot. Move to center court position and face the front wall. Do not play the return.

Success Goals = 10 out of 15 around-the-wall shots returned with both forehand and backhand strokes

Your Scores =

a. (#) _____ forehand shots returned out of 15

b. (#) _____ backhand shots returned out of 15

5. Game Situation

Play a game to 15 points. Score in the conventional manner, but give 2 bonus points whenever one player uses a Z-shot or an around-the-wall shot. Add these bonus points to score as they occur. Play three games.

Success Goal = Win 2 out of 3 games

Your Score = (#) _____ games won

Z-Shot and Around-the-Wall Shot Keys to Success Checklist

The key to using these shots is to remember to use them when you get pulled toward the front of the court. They can also be effective from deeper in the court when used as a change of pace. Have an observer watch you play a game. Be sure to hit lots of these shots so they can be evaluated using the Keys to Success items within Figure 17.3.

Step 18 Strategy Rule #6—Never Change a Winning Game, Always Change a Losing Game

This rule, like Rule #1, is simple and logical. Yet many players fail to recognize the importance of it. "If it ain't broke, don't fix it" is a phrase commonly heard in the sport world. This first half of the rule is usually the easiest to remember and utilize. But a slight letdown or change in strategy can be costly, so be alert to its significance. Changing a losing game is much harder to do. There is usually a valid reason why you are losing.

WHY IS STRATEGY RULE #6 IMPORTANT?

The value of this rule is that it should help you overcome negative thoughts and feelings. It should help you analyze the reasons for your lack of success. This in itself is a positive step in trying to change the outcome. Look at your strategy. Check yourself on Rules #1 through #5. Are you controlling the tempo or is your opponent? What is the reason? What shots should you discard? What shots haven't you been using? All these and more questions can help you change the direction and momentum of a game. The important thing is that you have done something. Often this process of analyzing and setting new goals is all that is necessary.

HOW TO EXECUTE STRATEGY RULE #6

Now is not the time to practice other shots or serves when you are winning. Continue to use the same strategy and shots that got you the lead. Momentum is a strange phenomenon in sports. When you have it, everything seems to go so easily. But when you lose it, it is extremely difficult to regain. Racquetball games are short, and the server can score many consecutive points in a row if they get hot. Don't give your opponent that chance.

A systematic look at a losing game is necessary for you to change the momentum. If your opponent is physically superior to you, nothing much can be done about that. If the problem is shot selection, position, or other strategy, often you can greatly improve your chances.

Receiving Position

Many times your position for receiving the serve almost guarantees success to the server. Do not overplay your backhand. You should be no more than one step to the backhand side of the midline. To be farther to the side leaves an opening to your forehand side and also puts you actually too close to your backhand corner. Many times you find the ball will be too close to you and you cannot extend your racquet arm to get a good swing at the ball. A bigger problem is that often receivers unconsciously move closer to the back wall on successive serves if they are not returning them. From a position where you can just touch the back wall with your outstretched racquet, take one or two steps toward the front wall. Otherwise, serves into either corner will give you trouble. Those that hit into the corner and come toward the midline will "handcuff" you by coming too close to you before you have a chance to adjust to them. You will not have time to move to get a full arm extension on your swing. Serves that hit the back wall and rebound sharply along the side wall will be too far away from you, and you probably will not be able to catch up to them. Rather, stay forward of the back wall. Then when the ball goes into the corner, you can turn and face the corner while watching for the direction of its rebound. Now you can go either way to get into position for your shot. A receiving position that is too deep is the number one cause of failure to return serves.

Returning Serves

Be prepared in advance with a backhand grip. Be sure to focus on the ball and not the server. Watch the ball from the time it is dropped until you play it. Try to think in advance what your options are. A ceiling shot is usually your best percentage return of most serves. Try to return it to the server's backhand. Don't be tempted to try a kill shot, especially on lob serves. This is a very low-percentage return. It should be attempted only by experts and then only if the server makes a poor serve. Remember, the server is in front of you and can rekill poor returns by you. The second-best-percentage shot is a passing shot. Down-the-line passes are best if the situation is right for one. Your main thought should be to put the serve into play. Then try to advance from making defensive shots to a center court position where you can then think of winning the rally.

Serving

When you are serving, be sure to change the types of serves and also their velocity and angles. Don't try to make that perfect ace serve every time. Usually when you try to hit your power serve too hard, you will make a fault. Better to get a good hard serve in and then look for a weak return to put away.

If you have a good power serve, learn to use it wisely. Changing your starting position by only a few inches can give different angles to the receiver, who may not even notice that you have served from a different position until it is too late. Changing the power slightly from one serve to the next can present more problems to the receiver. If a receiver starts returning your best serves regularly, these adjustments may help.

Try to develop skill with all the serves. This gives you not only a safe second serve but also the ability to change types of serves regularly, even on the first serve. The lob serve can be an effective first serve, especially if you are playing a power player who tries to kill everything.

During Play

If you find yourself running and your opponent occupying center court most of the time, ask yourself why. Are you trying offensive shots when your opponent is in front of you? Don't forget the ceiling shot. It's the greatest friend you have when momentum is against you.

Does your opponent kill your best kill attempts? Perhaps you are too predictable. Try some low passing shots once in a while in a kill situation.

Are you setting your opponent up off the back wall? Most players hit passing shots too hard. Take some power off so they die near the back wall. Nothing is more demoralizing to a player than to chase a passing shot toward the back wall only to have it die there before they can reach it.

Hitting Back Wall to Front Wall Returns

Do you find yourself hitting the ball hard into the back wall, hoping to return it to the front wall? This shot is usually executed with the forehand. It is a desperation shot and should never be attempted. It is usually a very weak return that your opponent can put away. Players need this shot for two reasons. The first reason is lack of an adequate backhand. Practice your backhand more, and keep using it in games. This way you will gradually develop confidence in your backhand. The second reason is related to the first—being caught out of position for the backhand. As soon as you start trying to return this shot with your backhand, your general court coverage and footwork will start to improve. It works the other way also. If you continue to hit this weak return, your court coverage and footwork will not improve.

Being Patient

Don't try to win all the points back in one rally. You can only win one point at a time. Get that one point first, then you can win another and another.

Using Strategy Rules Effectively

Are you working on your opponent's backhand? This might produce a weaker return and more time to set up and plan your next shot. Are you occupying center court regularly? If not, why not? What kind of shots will help you move your opponent out? Ceiling shots and good passing shots would be your best bet. Do you love the back wall? Let the ball go to the back wall. This could give you more time to set up and plan a quality shot. It also lets you locate your opponent. Are you hitting into the detour zone? If so, you are not making your opponent work hard enough. Are you honoring the "high–high, low–low" rule? If not, you are probably setting up your opponent too much. Try to make better quality shots. Substitute control for power to do this. Concentrate and make sure that the ball goes where you want it to go, regardless of how hard it is hit.

Detecting Errors in Using Strategy Rule #6

Errors in using this rule are mental. Sometimes you think only of how good your opponent is or how bad you are. You must stop thinking negative thoughts and start thinking positive ones. The only way to do this is to focus on some shots or strategy that you know will work. Here are some common errors and their solutions. Talk them over with your instructor or another friend. You may be surprised at what other people think about while they play.

ERROR

CORRECTION

1. You have difficulty returning serves.

2. Your serves are not effective.

1. Check your position. Be sure you have not backed up into the back wall. Plan several options you could use to return the next serve. Watch the ball and not the server's movement.

2. Be sure they are to the receiver's backhand. Seldom serve the same serve twice in a row. Change something, even if it's only the angle or velocity. Ask your instructor or a friend to observe your serves during a game and give you suggestions.

ERROR   **CORRECTION**

3. Your opponent always seems to control the rallies.

3. Use more ceiling shots and Z-shots. This will give you more time to get into position and plan your next shot. Vary the power on your shots. Don't always hit the ball as hard as you can. Try for better placement and less power. Plan your shot instead of just returning it to the front wall. Review the first five basic rules of strategy.

4. You have trouble thinking positive thoughts.

4. When you have a negative thought about your skill, try to think of a weakness of your opponent in a similar area. For example, if you have trouble returning a power serve to your backhand, think about how weak your opponent's backhand returns are. This helps you realize that everyone has weaknesses and that you can still win points in spite of your weakness.

5. You tend to give up when your opponent gets way ahead.

5. Try to set short-range goals. You can't score until you get the serve. Set a goal of taking the serve away. Set a goal of scoring two or three points in a row. You can't score 15 points at once—you score them one at a time. Short-range goals will help you try harder on each point. If your opponent is way ahead in the first game, try to score as many points as possible while using shots that will tire out your opponent for the following games.

Drills to Help You
Change a Losing Game

1. One-Point Game

Play a game to one point against an opponent. This will help you concentrate and focus on one point at a time. Play eight games, alternating turns at service.

Success Goal = Win 5 or more games

Your Score = (#) _____ games won

2. Two-Point Game

Play a game against an opponent. The receiver gets two points for winning the rally. The server gets one point for winning the rally. This will help you concentrate on trying to take the serve away from your opponent (short-range goal) instead of thinking about winning or losing the game. You can't score until you get the serve. Alternate every other serve. Play to seven points. Play as many games as time allows.

Success Goal = Win 50 percent or more of games played

Your Score = (%) _____ games won

3. Game Point

You are the receiver with the score 14-0 against you. Try to score five points before your opponent wins the game. This means you must take the serve away and score five points. If your opponent wins the game, reverse roles. This drill helps you overcome negative thoughts when you have game point against you. Instead of thinking about losing the game, you focus on something positive and realistic.

Success Goal = Score at least five points

Your Score = (#) _____ points scored

4. *Shot Selection Chart*

Study the chart shown in Figure 18.1 with a partner. Select one of the nine position combinations shown in the chart. Set up according to the positions selected. Play the ball, executing at least one correct shot as specified on the chart. Continue until all nine position combinations are played, then exchange roles with your partner.

Success Goal = 7 correct responses out of 9 position combinations played

Your Score = (#) _____ correct responses according to both you and your partner's position

Opponent's position ╲ Your position	Front court	Center court	Backcourt
Front court	Pass. *Do not kill.*	Cross-court pass, down-the-line pass, ceiling shot. *Do not kill.*	Down-the-line pass, cross-court pass, ceiling shot. *Do not kill.*
Center court	Drop kill, pinch kill, Z-shot, around-the-wall shot, down-the-line pass.	Pinch kill, down-the-line pass, ceiling shot, Z-shot, around-the-wall shot.	Down-the-line pass, cross-court pass, ceiling shot.
Backcourt	Pinch kill, drop kill, straight wall kill, inside corner kill.	Pinch kill, straight kill, inside corner kill, ceiling shot. *Do not pass.*	Ceiling shot, pinch kill, inside corner kill, straight wall kill occasionally. *Do not pass.*

Figure 18.1 Shot selection chart.

Rating Your Total Progress

Now that you have had some success in learning the basics of racquetball, rate yourself in each of the following categories using *Excellent*, *Good*, *Average*, or *Poor* to describe your performance progress:

	Excel	Good	Aver	Poor
Position for shots				
Foot and body position	_____	_____	_____	_____
Use of weak hand	_____	_____	_____	_____
Height of shots	_____	_____	_____	_____
Move with shot	_____	_____	_____	_____
Eyes on ball	_____	_____	_____	_____
Serves (quality and placement)				
Lob serve	_____	_____	_____	_____
Power serve	_____	_____	_____	_____
Z-serves	_____	_____	_____	_____
Uses variety of serves	_____	_____	_____	_____
Basic shots (quality and placement)				
Passing	_____	_____	_____	_____
Ceiling	_____	_____	_____	_____
Kill	_____	_____	_____	_____
Z-shot	_____	_____	_____	_____
Around-the-Wall	_____	_____	_____	_____
Defense (ability to return)				
Serves	_____	_____	_____	_____
Ceiling shots	_____	_____	_____	_____
Low shots on front wall	_____	_____	_____	_____
Shots to backhand	_____	_____	_____	_____
General strategy				
Change of speed—rallies	_____	_____	_____	_____
Change of speed—serves	_____	_____	_____	_____
Work on opponent's weaknesses	_____	_____	_____	_____
Drive opponent from offensive position	_____	_____	_____	_____
Move quickly to offensive position	_____	_____	_____	_____

	Excel	Good	Aver	Poor
Using the Six Strategy Rules				
Rule #1—Hit it to their backhand	_____	_____	_____	_____
Rule #2—I own center court	_____	_____	_____	_____
Rule #3—Love the back wall	_____	_____	_____	_____
Rule #4—Stay out of the detour zone	_____	_____	_____	_____
Rule #5—High–high, low–low	_____	_____	_____	_____
Rule #6—Never change a winning game, always change a losing game	_____	_____	_____	_____

Now review your rating of yourself. Pick out the areas where you need to improve. Review those steps for drills that will help you continue to improve.

Appendix

Individual Program

INDIVIDUAL COURSE IN _____ GRADE/COURSE SECTION _____

STUDENT'S NAME _____ STUDENT ID # _____

SKILLS/CONCEPTS	TECHNIQUE AND PERFORMANCE OBJECTIVES	WT* X	POINT PROGRESS** =				FINAL SCORE***
		%	1	2	3	4	

Note. From "The Role of Expert Knowledge Structures in an Instructional Design Model for Physical Education" by J.N. Vickers, 1983, *Journal of Teaching in Physical Education,* **2**(3), p. 17. Copyright 1983 by Joan N. Vickers. Adapted by permission.

*WT = Weighting of an objective's degree of difficulty.

**PROGRESS = Ongoing success, which may be expressed in terms of (a) accumulated points (1, 2, 3, 4); (b) grades (D, C, B, A); (c) symbols (merit, bronze, silver, gold); (d) unsatisfactory/satisfactory; and others as desired.

***FINAL SCORE equals WT times PROGRESS.

143

AARA—American Amateur Racquetball Association, the governing body of amateur racquetball (formerly the International Racquetball Association).

ace—A legal serve that eludes the receiver. One point is scored.

advantage position—Center court position; position from which kill and pass shots are best executed.

A player—A player whose skill level is very advanced. Sometimes used synonymously with *open player*. Varies locally.

around-the-wall shot—A defensive shot that hits a side wall, the front wall, and the other side wall, in that order, before touching the floor.

avoidable hinder—An interference with the opponent's play that could have been prevented or avoided; can be intentional or unintentional.

backcourt—The last 15 feet of the court, covering the area from the receiving line to the back wall.

backhand—A fundamental stroke hit across the body, starting on the side opposite the racquet hand. A right-hander's backhand stroke is from left to right across his or her body.

backhand corner—The area of the court where a side wall and the back wall meet; the same side as the player's backhand.

backhand grip—The way the hand grasps the racquet for the backhand stroke.

backswing—The preparatory part of a stroke in which the racquet is taken back to the ready position.

back wall—The rear wall of a court.

block—A court maneuver that prevents an opponent from viewing the ball. Also called a *screen*.

B player—A player whose skill level is average or intermediate. Varies locally.

bumper guard—A protective covering attached to the rim of the racquet head.

ceiling ball—A ball that hits the ceiling first, then the front wall (or reverse), rebounding to the backcourt.

ceiling return—A ceiling ball used as a service return.

choke—(1) To move the hand up or down on the racquet handle; (2) to panic during a match.

closed face—A racquet-face angle in which the hitting surface slants toward the floor or to the front wall side of a player.

corner shot—Any shot that hits at or near one of the two front corners.

court hinder—Deflection of the ball by an obstruction on the court, such as a door handle or light fixture (the point is replayed).

C player—A player whose skill level is at the basic or fundamental level; the advanced beginner level. Varies locally.

cross-court drive return—A relatively hard-hit service return that hits the front wall and passes the server on the side opposite from where the shot was hit.

cross-court passing shot—A passing shot hit from the left side of the court to the right, or from the right to the left.

crotch—The line juncture at which two flat surfaces of the court join. An example is the floor-side wall crotch.

crotch serve—An illegal serve that strikes the juncture of the front wall and the floor, ceiling, or side wall.

crotch shot—A shot that hits the juncture of any two playing surfaces.

cutthroat—A game involving three players in which the server plays against the other two players, with each player serving in turn.

dead ball—A ball that is no longer in play.

default—To lose a match by failing to show up or refusing to play.

defensive shot—A shot made to continue a rally, in an attempt to maneuver an opponent out of the center court position.

doubles—A game or match in which one team opposes another team; each team consists of two players.

down-the-line shot—A shot hit near a side wall that hits the front wall directly and then rebounds back along the same side wall.

drive—A powerfully hit ball that travels in a straight line.

drop shot—A shot hit with very little force, rebounding only a few feet from the front wall, usually hit into a corner.

eye guards—Special glasses or protectors worn to protect the eyes while playing racquetball.

fault—An illegal serve or infraction of the rules while serving. Two faults result in a side-out.

five-foot line—The broken line 5 feet behind and parallel to the short line. Also called the *receiving line*.

fly ball—Any shot taken before a floor bounce; hit directly on the rebound off the front or side wall; also called a *volley shot*.

follow-through—The continuation of the swing after contact is made with the ball.

forehand—A fundamental stroke hit across the body from the same side as the racquet hand. A right-hander's forehand stroke is from the right to left across her or his body.

four-wall racquetball—The most popular variety of the game, as opposed to three-wall or one-wall racquetball. In four-wall racquetball, the ball is played off the four walls, the ceiling, and the floor.

front court—The first 15 feet of the court, from the front wall to the service line.

front-wall kill—A kill shot that hits and rebounds off the front wall, touching neither side wall, and then returns so that the opponent is unable to retrieve it.

front wall–side wall kill—A kill shot that hits and rebounds off the front wall, touches either side wall, and rebounds in such a way that the opponent is unable to retrieve the ball; also called an *inside corner kill*.

game—The portion of a match that is completed when one player or team reaches 15 points.

grip—(1) The manner in which the racquet handle is grasped; (2) the cover material of the racquet that prevents slippage.

half and half—A method of positioning players for doubles and cutthroat; each player covers half the court, either the left or the right side.

half volley—Hitting the ball on the rise, just after it bounces off the floor; the shot resulting from this action.

hinder—An unintentional interference or screen of a ball so that the opponent does not have a fair chance to make a return. The point is replayed without penalty.

I formation—A method of positioning players for doubles and cutthroat; one player covers the front court, the other the backcourt; also called *up and back*.

live ball—(1) A ball still in play, as opposed to a dead ball; (2) a racquetball that is fast or has a high bounce.

lob shot—A shot that is hit high and gently toward the front wall and rebounds to the back wall in a high arc (often used as a serve).

long serve—A serve that rebounds to the back wall without hitting the floor. This is a fault.

match—A complete racquetball contest when one player wins two out of three games.

midcourt—The area of the court between the service line and the short serve line.

novice—A relatively low-skilled player or a true beginner at the sport; sometimes synonymous with *C player*.

offensive shot—Any shot intended either to end the rally immediately or to put the opponent in a weak court position; usually a kill or pass shot.

overhead—A shot hit at shoulder level or higher.

paddleball—Racquetball's immediate predecessor; played on the same court and with the same rules as racquetball, but a wooden paddle and different ball are used.

pass shot—A shot hit past an opponent out of her or his reach; may be cross-court or down-the-wall type. Also called a *drive shot*.

pinch shot—A kill shot that hits the side and front walls near the corner.

power serve—A hard-hit serve where the ball rebounds fast to the backcourt; also called a *drive serve*.

rally—An exchange of shots after the serve that is continued until play ends.

ready position—A stance taken by a player while waiting for a serve or shot.

receiving line—The 5-foot line.

referee—The person who makes all judgment calls in tournament play.

rollout—A shot in which the ball rolls out on the floor after rebounding off the front wall. A sure point, because it is impossible to retrieve.

safety hinder—The interruption of a rally when continued play could cause an injury. The point is replayed.

serve—The act of putting the ball in play.

server—The player who puts the ball in play.

serve return—The shot used to return the ball after the serve.

service zone—The court area between the short line and the service line, from side wall to side wall, where the server must stand while serving.

setup—A potential shot during the rally that should be an easy scoring opportunity for the hitter.

short line—The back line of the service zone that divides the court into equal halves.

side-by-side formation—A method of player positioning in doubles and cutthroat. Each player covers half of the court, either the left or the right side. Also called *half and half*.

side-out—The loss of a serve to the opponent or other team; usually simply referred to as an *out* in singles.

singles—A racquetball game in which one player opposes another player.

skip ball—A return that hits the floor before reaching the front wall.

straddle ball—Any shot that passes through the legs of one of the players after the front wall rebound; this is a hinder only if it visually or physically impedes the other player from hitting the ball.

straight kill—See *front-wall kill*.

thong—A strap attached to a racquet and worn around the player's wrist. The strap must be fastened securely to eliminate the possibility of the racquet flying out of the player's hands.

three-wall serve—An illegal serve that strikes three walls before hitting the floor; a serve striking the front wall, side wall, and opposite wall; counts as one service fault.

throat—The part of the racquet between the strings and the grip.

unavoidable hinder—Accidental interference with an opponent or the flight of the ball. No penalty is suffered, and the rally is replayed.

volley—To hit the ball on the fly before it bounces. This is legal both on the serve return and during the rally. Also called a *fly shot*.

wallpaper shot—A shot that stays very close to the side wall; difficult to return.

winner—A successful shot that results in a point or side-out.

Suggested Readings

Allsen, P., & Witbeck, A. (1977). *Racquetball* (4th ed.). Dubuque, IA: Brown.

Collins, D.R., Hodges, P., & Marshall, M. (1985). *The art and science of racquetball* (2nd ed.). Bloomington, IN: Tichenor.

Fabian, L. (1986). *Racquetball: Strategies for winning*. Dubuque, IA: Eddie Bowers.

Stafford, R. (1990). *Racquetball: The sport for everyone* (3rd ed.). Memphis: Stafford.

Turner, E., & Hogan, M. (1988). *Skills and strategies for winning raquetball*. Champaign, IL: Leisure Press.

Verner, B. (1985). *Racquetball* (2nd ed.). Palo Alto, CA: Mayfield.

About the Author

Stan Kittleson is an accomplished racquetball player and has been teaching racquetball since 1972. He has been a physical educator in college settings since 1968. He earned his PhD from the University of Illinois in 1973. Dr. Kittleson has served as president of the Illinois Association for Professional Preparation in Health, Physical Education, and Recreation and is a member of the American Alliance for Health, Physical Eduction, Recreation and Dance (AAHPERD). He is currently a professor of physical education at Augustana College in Rock Island, Illinois. When not teaching or playing racquetball, Dr. Kittleson enjoys scuba diving, alpine skiing, and golf.